SWU-700-009

UNIFORMS OF RUSSIAN ARMY IN THE XVIII CENT. VOL.2

UNDER THE REIGN OF CATHERINE II
EMPRESSE OF RUSSIA BETWEEN 1762 AND 1796

From the Viskovatov's greatest work:
"Historical description of the clothing and
arms of the Russian Army"

SOLDIERSHOP PUBLISHING

AUTHOR

Aleksandr Vasilevich Viskovatov born 22 April (4 May New Style) 1804, died 27 February (11 March) 1858 in St. Petersburg, Russian military historian. He graduated from the 1st Cadet Corps and served in the artillery, the hydrographic depot of the Naval Ministry, and then in the Department of Military Educational Institutions. He mainly studied historical artifacts and the histories of military units. Viskovatov's greatest work was the Historical Description of the Clothing and Arms of the Russian Army.

Title: **UNIFORMS OF RUSSIAN ARMY IN THE XVIII Cent. VOL. 2 -**
The Russian Army under the reign of Catherine the Great 1762-1796
By A.V.Viskovatov. Serie edit by Luca S. Cristini. First edition by Soldiershop. March 2017
Cover & Art Design: Luca S. Cristini. Plates re-colorations by Anna Cristini.
ISBN code: 978-88-93272315
Published by Soldiershop publishing, via Padre Davide, 7 - 24050 Zanica (BG) ITALY. www.soldiershop.com

SOLDIERSHOP
PUBLISHING
BOOK on DEMAND

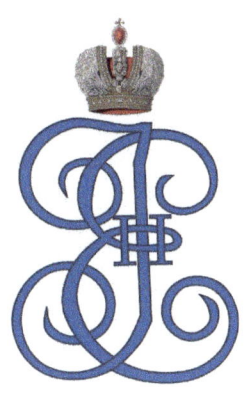

UNIFORMS
OF THE RUSSIAN ARMY IN
THE XVIII Cent.
VOL. 2

UNDER THE REIGN OF CATHERINE II EMPRESSE OF
RUSSIA BETWEEN 1762 AND 1796

Catherine II of Russia also known as Catherine the Great 21 April 1729 – 6 November 1796) by F. Rokotov after Roslin (c.1770, Hermitage)

HISTORICAL DESCRIPTION OF THE CLOTHING AND ARMS OF THE RUSSIAN ARMY - A.V. VISKOVATOV

Soldiershop is glad to presents the complete collection of the great job made by A.V. Viskovatov dedicated to the uniforms and weapons belonging from the first Zar and Russian emperors to the Russian army during the Napoleonic period, until 1860 about. The time we considered in this volume corresponds to the reigns of Catherine the Great (Catherine II) who reigned since 1762 until his murder on the 6 November 1796.

Our reprint in based on the original 19ᵗʰ century volumes, to be precise the volumes from 4 to 6 are dedicated to the reign of Catherine II; this part is distributed on 3 or 4 volumes.

Our new edition, the first ever published in English, both on paper and digital format, boasts a large number of color plates, many of them unpublished and re-coloured by our team of expert artists and scholars of uniformology. Each volume is based on 100 color plates or more, always accompanied by the original translated text which describes the subjets of the plates.

A unique work in its genre, a must have in any respecting collection!

Aleksandr Vasilevich Viskovatov born 22 April (4 May New Style) 1804, died 27 February (11 March) 1858 in St. Petersburg, Russian military historian. He graduated from the 1st Cadet Corps and served in the artillery, the hydrographic depot of the Naval Ministry, and then in the Department of Military Educational Institutions.

He mainly studied historical artifacts and the histories of military units. Viskovatov's greatest work was the Historical Description of the Clothing and Arms of the Russian Army (Vols. 1-30, St. Petersburg, 1841-62; 2nd ed. Vols. 1-34, St. Petersburg - Novosibirsk - Leningrad, 1899-1948). This work is based on a great quantity of archival documents and contains four thousand colored illustrations.

Viskovatov was the author of Chronicles of the Russian Army (Books 1-20, St. Petersburg, 1834-42) and Chronicles of the Russian Imperial Army (Parts 1-7, St. Petersburg, 1852). He collected valuable material on the history of the Russian navy which went into A Short Overview of Russian Naval Campaigns and General Voyages to the End of the XVII Century (St. Petersburg, 1864; 2nd edition Moscow, 1946). Together with A.I. Mikhailovskii-Danilevskii he helped prepare and create the Military Gallery in the Winter Palace.

He wrote the historical military inscriptions for the walls of the Hall of St. George in the Great Palace of the Kremlin. (From the article in the Soviet Military Encyclopedia.)

CONTENTS

*

MEMOIRS OF THE EMPRESS CATHERINE II
WRITTEN BY HERSELF - PART II.

SECOND PART: FROM 1751, TO 1754

On the 15th of December we left Moscow for St. Petersburg, travelling night and day in an open sledge. About midway I was again seized with a violent toothache. Notwithstanding this, the Grand Duke would not consent to close the sledge: scarcely would he allow me to draw the curtain a little, so as to shelter me from a cold and damp wind, blowing right into my face. At last we reached Zarskoe-Selo, where the Empress had already arrived, having passed us on the road, according to her usual custom. As soon as I stepped out of the sledge I entered the apartment destined for us, and sent for her Majesty's physician Boërhave, the nephew of the celebrated Boërhave, requesting him to have the tooth which had tormented me so much for the last four or five months extracted.

He consented with great reluctance, and only because I absolutely insisted on it. At last he sent for Gyon, my surgeon: I sat on the ground, Boërhave on one side, Tchoglokoff on the other, and Gyon drew the tooth; but the moment he did so, my eyes, nose, and mouth became fountains, whence poured out—from my mouth, blood, from my eyes and nose water. Boërhave, who was a man of clear and sound judgment, instantly exclaimed, "Clumsy!" and calling for the tooth, he added, "I feared it would be so, and that was why I did not wish it to be drawn." Gyon, in extracting the tooth, had carried away with it a portion of the lower jaw, to which it was attached.

At this moment the Empress came to the door of my room, and I was afterwards told that she was moved even to tears. I was put to bed, and suffered a great deal during four weeks, even in the city, whither we went next day, notwithstanding all this, and still in open sleighs. I did not leave my room till the middle of January, 1750, for the lower part of my cheek still bore in blue and yellow stains, the impression of the five fingers of M. Gyon. On new-year's day this year wishing to have my hair dressed, I noticed that the young man who was to do it, a Kalmuck whom I had trained for this purpose, was excessively red, and his eyes very piercing. I asked what was the matter, and learned that he had a very bad headache and great heat. I sent him away, desiring him to go to bed, for indeed he was not fit to do anything. He retired, and in the evening I was informed that the small-pox had broken out upon him. I escaped with nothing worse than the fright which this gave me, for I did not catch the disease, although he had combed my hair.

The Empress remained at Zarskoe-Selo during a considerable portion of the Carnival. Petersburg was nearly deserted, for most of its residents lived there from necessity rather than choice. While the court was at Moscow, and also when on its return to St. Petersburg, all the courtiers were eager to obtain leave of absence for a year, six months, or even a few weeks. The officials, such as senators, and others, did the same; and when they were afraid of not succeeding, then came the illnesses, real or feigned, of husbands, wives, fathers, brothers, mothers, sisters, or children; or lawsuits, or other business which it was indispensable to settle. In a word, it sometimes took six months, or even more, before the court and the city became what they were previously to one of these absences; and when the court was away, the grass grew in the streets of St. Petersburg, for there were scarcely any carriages in the city.

In such a state of things, at the present moment, there was not much company to be expected, especially by us who were so much shut up. M. Tchoglokoff thought to amuse us during this time, or rather to amuse himself and his wife, by inviting us to play at cards with him in the apartments which he occupied at court, and which consisted of four or five rather small rooms. He also invited there the ladies and gentlemen in waiting, and the Princess of Courland, daughter of Duke Ernest John Biren, the ancient favourite of the Empress Anne. The Empress Elizabeth had recalled this Duke from Siberia, whither he had been exiled under the regency of the Princess Anne. There, the Duke was living with his wife, his sons, and his daughter. This daughter was neither handsome nor pretty, nor well made, for she was humpbacked, and rather small; but she had fine eyes, much intelligence, and a singular talent for intrigue.

Her parents were not very fond of her; she pretended, indeed, that they constantly ill-treated her. One day she fled from home, and took refuge with the wife of the Waiwode of Yaroslav, Madame Pouchkine. This woman, delighted to have an opportunity of giving herself importance at court, took her to Moscow, addressed herself to Madame Schouvaloff, and the flight of the Princess of Courland from her father's house was represented as the result of the ill-treatment she had received from her parents, in consequence of her having expressed a desire to embrace the religion of the Greek church. In fact, the first thing she did at court was to make her profession of faith.

The Empress stood godmother for her, after which she received an appointment among the maids of honour. M. Tchoglokoff made it a point to show her attention, because her elder brother had laid the foundation of his fortune, by taking him from the corps of cadets, where he was receiving his education, removing him into the horse-guards, and keeping him about himself as a messenger. The Princess of Courland thus brought into our society, and playing daily for hours at trisset with the Grand Duke, Tchoglokoff, and myself, conducted herself at first with great discretion.

She was insinuating, and her intelligence made one forget what was disagreeable in her figure, especially when seated. She adapted her conversation to the character of her auditors, speaking to each in the manner most likely to be agreeable. Every one looked upon her as an interesting orphan, and a person not likely to be in any one's way.

In the eyes of the Grand Duke she had another merit, and no slight one either—she was a sort of foreign Princess, and, what was more, a German; he therefore always spoke to her in German, and this gave her a charm in his eyes.

He began to pay her as much attention as he was capable of doing. When she dined alone, he sent her wine, as well as favourite dishes from his table, and when he got hold of some new grenadier's cap or shoulder-belt, he sent them to her to look at. The Princess of Courland, who at that time might be about four or five and twenty, was not the only acquisition made by the court at Moscow. The Empress had then taken the two Countesses Voronzoff, nieces of the Vice-Chancellor, and daughters of Count Roman Voronzoff, his younger brother. Mary, the elder, might be about fourteen; she was placed among the Empress' maids of honour. The younger sister, Elizabeth, was only eleven; she was given to me. She was a very ugly child, of an olive complexion, and excessively slovenly. Towards the end of the Carnival, her Majesty returned to town, and in the first week of Lent we began to prepare for our duty. On the Wednesday evening I was to take a bath at the house of Madame Tchoglokoff, but on Tuesday evening she came to my room, and told the Grand Duke, who was with me, that it was her Majesty's pleasure that he also should take a bath.

Now the baths, and all other Russian customs and habits, were not simply disagreeable to the Duke, he had a mortal hatred for them. He therefore unceremoniously declared that he would do nothing of the kind. She, who was equally obstinate, and had no kind of reserve or ceremony in her speech, told him that this was an act of disobedience to her Imperial Majesty. He maintained that he ought not to be required to do what was repugnant to his nature; that he knew that the bath, in which he had never been, was unsuitable to his constitution; that he did not want to die; that life was the thing he held most dear, and that her Majesty should never compel him to go into the bath. Madame Tchoglokoff replied that her Majesty would know how to punish his disobedience.

At this he became angry, and exclaimed, passionately, "I should like to see what she can do; I am not a child."

Madame Tchoglokoff threatened that the Empress would send him to the Fortress. At this he cried bitterly; and they went on answering each other in the most outrageous terms that passion could dictate; in fact, they both acted as if they had not between them a grain of common sense. At last, Madame Tchoglokoff departed, saying that she would report the conversation to her Imperial Majesty word for word. I know not what she did in the matter, but she returned presently with an entirely different theme, for she came to inform us that her Imperial Majesty was very angry that we had no children, and wished to know which of us was in fault; that she would therefore send a midwife to me, and a physician to the Grand Duke. To this she added various other outrageous remarks—remarks which had neither head nor tail, and concluded by saying that her Majesty had dispensed with our going to our duty this week, because the Grand Duke said the bath was injurious to his health. I must state that during these two conversations I never once opened my lips; in the first place, because they both spoke with such vehemence that I could find no chance of putting in a word; secondly, because I saw that both of them were utterly unreasonable. I do not know what view the Empress took of the matter, but, at all events, nothing more was said on either topic.

About mid-Lent, her Majesty went to Gostilitza, to the residence of Count Razoumowsky, to celebrate his feast, and we were sent, together with her maids of honour and our ordinary suite, to Zarskoe-Selo. The weather was wonderfully mild, even warm, so that, on the 17th of March, instead of there being snow on the road, there was dust.

Having established ourselves at Zarskoe-Selo, the Grand Duke and Tchoglokoff recommenced their hunting; I and the ladies walked or drove out as long as we could, and in the evening we all played at various small games. Here the Grand Duke manifested a decided partiality for the Princess of Courland, especially when he had been drinking in the evening—a thing which happened every day. He was always at her side, and spoke to no one but her. At last this thing went on in the most glaring manner, before my eyes, and before every one, so that my vanity and self-love began to be shocked at finding myself slighted for the sake of a little, deformed creature like this.

One evening, on rising from table, Madame Vladislava said to me that every one was disgusted to see this little hunchback preferred to me. "It cannot be helped," I said, as the tears started to my eyes. I went to bed; scarcely was I asleep when the Grand Duke also came to bed. As he was tipsy, and knew not what he was doing, he spoke to me for the purpose of expatiating on the eminent qualities of his favourite. To check his garrulity as soon as possible, I pretended to be fast asleep. He spoke still louder in order to wake me, but finding that I still slept, he gave me two or three rather hard blows in the side with his fist; then, growling at the heaviness of my slumbers, he turned on his side and dropped asleep himself. I wept long and bitterly that night, as well on account of the matter itself, and the blows he had given me, as on that of my general situation, which was in all respects as disagreeable as it was wearisome.

In the morning, the Duke seemed ashamed of what he had done; he did not speak of it, and I acted as if I had not felt anything. Two days afterwards we returned to town. The last week of Lent we recommenced our preparations for going to our duty. Nothing more was said to the Duke about the bath.

Another occurrence took place this week which perplexed him a little. While in his room he was nearly always in constant movement of one sort or other. One afternoon he was exercising himself in cracking an immense coachman's whip, which he had had made for him. He whipped about right and left, and made his valets jump from one corner to another, fearing to come in for a chance slash. At last he somehow contrived to give himself a severe blow on the cheek. The mark extended all along the left side of his face, and the blow was severe enough to make the blood start.

He was very much disturbed, fearing that he should not be able to go out even by Easter; that the Empress should again forbid him to communicate, as his face was bloody; and that when she came to learn the cause of the accident, he should get some disagreeable reprimand for his whipping amusements. He instantly ran to consult me, as he always did in such emergencies. Seeing him enter with his cheek all bloody, I exclaimed, "Good heavens! what has happened to you?" He told me. Having thought a little, I said, "Well, perhaps I can manage the matter for you; but, first of all, go to your room, and try if possible to prevent your cheek from being seen by any one. I will come to you as soon as I have got what I want, and I trust we shall so manage that no one will be the wiser."

He went off, and I recollected a preparation which had served me some years before in a similar predicament.

I had a fall in the garden at Peterhoff, and took the skin off my face so that it bled; my surgeon Gyon gave me some white lead in the form of pomade, and I covered the wound with it, and went out as usual, without any one having perceived that I had scratched myself. I now sent for this pomade, and having received it, I went to the Grand Duke, and dressed his face so well, that he could not detect anything himself by looking in the glass. On the Thursday we received the communion, in company with the Empress, in the great church of the court, and then returned to our places.

The light fell on the Grand Duke's cheek. Tchoglokoff approached for some purpose or other, and looking at the Duke, said, "Wipe your cheek, there is some pomatum on it." Instantly, as if in jest, I said to the Grand Duke, "And I, who am your wife, forbid your doing it." The Grand Duke, turning to Tchoglokoff, said, "See how these women treat us; we dare not even wipe our faces, if they do not like it." Tchoglokoff laughed, saying, "Well, this is indeed a woman's caprice!"

The matter rested there, and the Duke felt grateful to me as well for the pomade which had spared him unpleasant results, as for my presence of mind, which had prevented all suspicion even in the case of M. Tchoglokoff.

As I had to be up before daylight on Easter morning, I went to bed about five o'clock in the afternoon of Holy Saturday, intending to sleep till the time arrived for dressing. Scarcely had I got into bed when the Duke came running in in a violent hurry, telling me to make haste and get up to eat some fresh oysters, which had just been brought to him from Holstein. This was a great and double treat for him; first, because he was fond of oysters, and, secondly, because they came from Holstein, his native country, for which he had a great love, though he did not govern it any the better for that; for he both did, and was made to do, terrible things in it, as will be seen in the sequel. Not to get up would have been to disoblige him, and risk a serious quarrel; I therefore rose, dressed myself, and went to his apartments, though I was very much fatigued by the devotional exercises of the Holy Week. When I reached his room, I found the oysters served. Having eaten a dozen of them, I was allowed to return to bed, while he continued his repast.

Indeed, he was all the better pleased by my not eating too many, as there were more left for himself, for he was excessively greedy in the matter of oysters. At midnight I got up, and dressed myself for the matins and mass of Easter Sunday; but I could not remain till the end of the service, for I was seized with a violent cholic. I never remember having had such severe pains. I returned to my room with no one but the Princess Gagarine, all my people being in church. She assisted me to undress and get into bed, and sent for the doctors. I took medicine, and kept my bed during the first two days of the festival.

It was a little before this time that Count Bernis, Ambassador from the Court of Vienna, Count Lynar, the Envoy of Denmark, and General Arnheim, Envoy of Saxony, arrived in Russia. The latter brought with him his wife, who was by birth of the family of Hoim. Count Bernis was a native of Piedmont; he was intellectual, amiable, gay, and well educated, and of such a disposition that, although more than fifty years of age, young people preferred his society to that of persons of their own age. He was generally loved and esteemed, and I have a thousand times said, that if he, or some one like him, had been placed with the Grand Duke, the most beneficial results would have followed, for the Duke as well as myself had a very great regard and affection for him. In fact, the Duke said himself, that with such a man near, a person would be ashamed of doing anything wrong or foolish—an excellent remark, which I have never forgotten.

Count Bernis had with him, as attaché, Count Hamilton, a Knight of Malta. One day, when I made inquiries of this gentleman about the health of the Ambassador Count Bernis, who was indisposed, it occurred to me to say that I had the highest opinion of Count Bathyani, whom the Empress-Queen had just named tutor to her two elder sons, the Archdukes Joseph and Charles, since she had preferred him for this office to Count Bernis. In the year 1780, when I had my first interview with the Emperor Joseph II. at Mohilev, his Imperial Majesty told me that he was aware I had made this remark. I replied that he must have learnt this from Count Hamilton, who had been placed with him on his return from Russia. He then said that I had surmised correctly in the case of Count Bathyani; for Count Bernis, whom he had not known, had left the reputation of being better suited to the office than his old tutor.

Count Lynar, the Envoy of the King of Denmark, had been sent to Russia to treat of the exchange of Holstein, which belonged to the Grand Duke, for the country of Oldenburg. He was, according to report, a person of much information, and of no less capacity. His appearance was that of a most complete fop. He was tall and well made, his hair fair with a tinge of red, and his complexion as delicately white as a woman's. It was said that he took such care of his skin, that he never went to bed without covering his face and hands with pomade, and also that he wore gloves and a mask at night. He boasted of having eighteen children, and pretended that he had always put the nurses of those children in the condition of continuing their vocation. This white Count wore the white order of Denmark, and dressed in the lightest colours; such as sky-blue, apricot, lilac, flesh colour, &c., although such light shades were, at that time, rarely worn by men. The High Chancellor, Count Bestoujeff, and his wife, treated him with the most marked favour.

He was received at their house as one of the family, and greatly fêted. This, however, did not shelter him from ridicule. There was also another point against him, viz., that it was not forgotten that his brother had been more than well-received by the Princess Anne, whose regency had been disapproved of. The Count had hardly arrived when he announced the object of his mission, which was, to negotiate an exchange of the duchy of Holstein for the territory of Oldenburg.

The High Chancellor sent for M. Pechlin, minister of the Grand Duke for his duchy of Holstein, and told him the purport of Count Lynar's mission. M. Pechlin made his report to the Grand Duke. The Duke was passionately attached to his country of Holstein. From the period of our stay in Moscow, it had been represented to her Imperial Majesty as insolvent. He had asked her for money for it, and she had given him a little, but it had never reached Holstein; it went to pay the clamorous debts of his Imperial Highness in Russia. M. Pechlin represented the affairs of Holstein, as far as pecuniary considerations were concerned, as desperate. This was easy for him to do, as the Grand Duke depended upon him for the administration, and gave the matter but little or no attention himself; so that, on one occasion, Pechlin, quite out of patience, said to him, in slow and measured accents, "My Lord, it depends on a sovereign to give his attention to the government of his country, or not to do so. If he does not attend to it, the country governs itself, but it governs itself badly." This Pechlin was a very short, fat man, wearing an immense wig, but he was not deficient either in acquirements or capacity. This heavy and short body enclosed a subtle and shrewd spirit; he was accused, however, of not being over-delicate in his choice of means. The High Chancellor had great confidence in him; indeed, he was one of the persons most in his confidence. M. Pechlin represented to the Duke that to listen was not to negotiate, and that negotiation, also, was a very different thing from acceptance, and that he would always have it in his power to break off the negotiation when he thought proper. At last, step by step, they got him to consent that M. Pechlin should listen to the propositions of the Danish minister, and thus the negotiation was opened. The Grand Duke was distressed, and spoke to me on the subject. I, who had been brought up in the ancient hatred of the house of Holstein against Denmark, and had constantly heard it averred that the projects of Count Bestoujeff were all directed against the interests of the Grand Duke and myself,

I, of course, could not hear of this project without impatience and anxiety. I opposed it to the Grand Duke as much as I could. No one, however, except himself, ever mentioned the subject to me, and to him the utmost secrecy had been recommended, especially in regard to women. I believe this caution had more reference to me than to any one else, but they were deceived in their expectations; for the Duke was always eager to tell me everything about it.

The more the negotiations advanced, the more did they endeavour to present the matter in an agreeable aspect to him. I often found him delighted at the prospect of what he should have, but then came revulsions of bitter regret for what he was going to lose. When they saw him hesitating, they relaxed the conferences, and only renewed them when they had invented some new bait for making him see things in a favourable light.

In the beginning of the spring we moved to the Summer Garden, and occupied the little house built by Peter I, the apartments of which are on a level with the garden. The stone quay, and the bridge of the Fontanka, had not then been built. In this house I had one of the most painful annoyances which I experienced during the entire reign of the Empress Elizabeth. One morning I was informed that the Empress had removed from my service my old valet de chambre, Timothy Yevreinoff. The pretext for this removal was, that Yevreinoff had had a quarrel, in a wardrobe chamber, with a man who used to bring us in coffee. Of this quarrel the Grand Duke had been in part a witness, having gone into the room while they were arguing, and heard a portion of their mutual abuse. The antagonist of Yevreinoff complained to M. Tchoglokoff, saying that Yevreinoff, without regard to the presence of the Grand Duke, had used most abusive language to him. M. Tchoglokoff immediately made his report to the Empress, who ordered both of them to be dismissed from the court, and Yevreinoff was sent off to Kasan, where he was subsequently made master of police. The truth of the matter was, that both men were very much attached to us, especially Yevreinoff, and this was but a pretext for depriving me of him. He had charge of everything belonging to me. The Empress ordered that a man named Skourine, whom he had taken in as an assistant, should take his place. In this person I had, at the time, no confidence.

After some stay in the house of Peter I, we were ordered to the Summer Palace, which was built of wood. Here new apartments had been prepared for us, one side of which faced the Fontanka, then a muddy marsh, while the other opened on a miserable and narrow yard. On Whit-Sunday, the Empress sent me word to invite Madame d'Arnheim, the wife of the Saxon Envoy, to accompany me. She was a tall woman, very well made, about five-and-twenty or six-and-twenty years of age, rather thin, and anything but handsome, for she was much and deeply marked by the small-pox; but, as she dressed well, she had, at some distance, a good appearance, and looked tolerably fair.

She arrived at about five o'clock in the afternoon, dressed like a man, from head to foot, her coat being of red cloth, bordered with gold lace, and her vest of green gros de Tours, similarly trimmed. She did not seem to know what to do with her hat or her hands, and appeared to us rather awkward. As I knew the Empress did not like my riding as a man, I had had made for me a lady's saddle, in the English style, and an English riding habit, of a rich azure and silvered cloth, with crystal buttons, which admirably imitated diamonds, while my black cap was surrounded with a string of diamonds. I went down stairs to mount my horse. At this moment the Empress came to our apartments to see us set off. As I was then very active, and accustomed to this exercise, as soon as I reached my horse I leaped into the saddle, my petticoat, which was open, falling on each side. The Empress seeing me mount with such agility and address, cried out in astonishment, and said it was impossible to have done better. She asked what kind of saddle I was using, and having learned that it was a side-saddle, she said, "One might have sworn it was a man's saddle." When Madame d'Arnheim's turn came, her skill did not shine very conspicuously in the eyes of her Imperial Majesty.

Her own horse had been led from her house. It was a large, heavy, black and ugly-looking animal, and our courtiers pretended that it must have been one of the leaders of her carriage. In order to mount, she was obliged to have the aid of steps, and the ceremony was not effected without a deal of fuss, and the assistance of several people. When mounted, the animal broke into a rough trot, which considerably shook the lady, who was neither firm in her seat nor in her stirrups, so that she had to hold on by the saddle. Seeing her mounted, I took the lead, and then—let those follow who could.

I overtook the Duke, who was a-head of me, and Madame d'Arnheim was left behind. I was told that the Empress laughed heartily, and was not at all pleased with Madame d'Arnheim's mode of riding. At last, after losing, now her hat and then her stirrups, she was picked up, I believe, some distance from the court, by Madame Tchoglokoff, who was in a carriage. Finally, she was brought to us at Catherinhoff; but the adventure was not yet ended. It had rained during the day, up to three o'clock in the afternoon, and the steps leading to Catherinhoff House were covered with pools of water.

After dismounting, I remained for some time in the hall, where a good deal of company had assembled. Then, wishing to reach the room where my women were, I thought I would go by these open steps. Madame d'Arnheim must needs follow me, and as I walked quickly, she was obliged to run. She thus stepped into these puddles, lost her footing, slipped, and fell flat upon the ground, amidst the laughter of the crowd of spectators gathered about the steps.

She got up, a little confused, laying the blame on the new boots she had put on that afternoon. We returned from this excursion in a carriage, and, on the way, Madame d'Arnheim entertained us with a detail of the good qualities of her steed; we had to bite our lips to prevent a burst of laughter. In a word, for many days she furnished a subject of merriment to the whole court and town. My women asserted that she had fallen from trying to imitate me, without being equally nimble; and Madame Tchoglokoff, who was by no means given to mirth, used to laugh till the tears came into her eyes, whenever any allusion was made to the subject, and this for a long time afterwards.

From the Summer Palace we went to Peterhoff, where, this year, we resided at Monplaisir. We regularly spent a portion of our afternoons at the residence of Madame Tchoglokoff, where, as there was always company, we were tolerably well amused. From Peterhoff we went to Oranienbaum, where we hunted whenever the weather permitted, being sometimes thirteen hours a-day in the saddle. The summer, however, was rather wet.

I remember one day, when returning home quite wet, that, as I was dismounting, I met my tailor, who said to me, "When I see you in this condition, I am not at all surprised that I can scarcely keep you in riding habits, and that new ones are continually required." The only material I wore for this purpose was silk camlet. The rain made it split, the sun faded the colours, so that I was obliged to have a constant succession of new habits.

It was during this time that I contrived for myself saddles on which I could sit in any way I pleased. They had the English crook, and yet the leg could be passed over, so as to ride like a man. Besides, the crook divided, and a second stirrup could be let down or raised at pleasure. If the equeries were asked how I was mounted, they said, "Upon a lady's saddle," according to the wishes of the Empress. I never passed my leg over except I felt quite sure of not being betrayed; and as I made no boast of my invention, while, besides, my attendants were anxious to please me, no inconvenience resulted.

The Grand Duke cared very little how I was mounted, while the equeries thought I ran less risk in riding astride, especially as I was constantly in the chase, than I did in sitting on the English saddles, which they detested, as they were always apprehensive of some accident, the blame of which they would, in all probability, have to bear. For myself, I cared little for the chase, but I was passionately fond of riding; and the more violent the exercise, the more I liked it, so that if a horse happened to run away, I was sure to be after it and bring it back. At that period, also, I had always a book in my pocket, and if I had a moment to myself, I spent it in reading.

I noticed, in these huntings, that M. Tchoglokoff became a good deal softened in his manners, especially towards me. This made me fear that he might take it into his head to pay his court to me—a thing which would not have suited me in any manner. In the first place, I did not at all like him. He was fair and foppish, very stout, and as heavy in mind as in body. He was universally hated, while he was in no respect agreeable. His wife's jealousy and his own malignity were equally to be feared, especially for one like me, who had nothing in the world to depend on but myself and my merit, if I had any. I therefore evaded, and very skilfully, I fancy, all the attentions of M. Tchoglokoff, without ever giving him any room for charging me with a want of politeness. All this was perfectly seen through by his wife, who felt grateful for it, and subsequently became much attached to me, partly, as will be seen in the sequel, from this cause.

There were in our court two chamberlains named Soltikoff, sons of the Adjutant-General Vasili Teodorovitch Soltikoff, whose wife, Mary Alexceëvna, born Princess Galitzine, the mother of these two young men, was very much esteemed by the Empress, on account of the signal services she had rendered her at the time of her accession to the throne, having on that occasion given proofs of a rare fidelity and attachment. Sergius, the younger of these sons, had been for some little time married to one of the Empress' maids of honour, named Matrena Pavlovna Balk. The elder brother was named Peter. He was a fool in the fullest sense of the word. He had the most stupid physiognomy I have ever seen, great staring eyes, a flat nose, and a mouth always half open; added to which he was a notorious tale-bearer, and as such welcome to the Tchoglokoffs, at whose house it was that Madame Vladislava, in virtue of an old acquaintance with the mother of this sort of imbecile, suggested to the Tchoglokoffs the idea of marrying him to the Princess of Courland. In consequence, he placed himself in the ranks as a suitor, proposed to her and obtained her consent, while his parents demanded that of the Empress. The Grand Duke knew nothing of all this until everything had been settled, that is, till our return to town. He was very much annoyed, and very much out of humour with the Princess. I do not know what excuse she gave him, but, although he disapproved of her marriage, she continued for a long time to retain a portion of his affection, and some degree of influence with him. As for me, I was delighted with this marriage, and had a superb dress embroidered for the intended. These court marriages, requiring the consent of the Empress, never took place till after years of delay, because her Majesty herself fixed the day, forgot it, often for a long time, and, when reminded of it, put it off from time to time. This was the case in the present instance. We returned then to town in autumn, and I had the satisfaction of seeing the Princess of Courland and M. Soltikoff thank her Majesty for the consent she had been graciously pleased to give to their union. After all, the family of Soltikoff was one of the oldest and noblest in the empire. It was even allied to the imperial family through the mother of the Empress Anne, who was a Soltikoff, but of a different branch to the one in question; while M. Biren, created Duke of Courland by the favour of the Empress Anne, was the son of a petty farmer on the estate of a gentleman in Courland. The name of this farmer was Biren; but the favour enjoyed by the son in Russia induced the Birons of France, at the persuasion of Cardinal Fleury, to acknowledge him; for Fleury, anxious to gain over the court of Russia, favoured the views and vanity of Biren, Duke of Courland.

On arriving in town, we learnt that besides the two days a-week set apart for French plays, there would also be, twice a-week, a masquerade ball. The Grand Duke added another day for concerts in his own apartments, and on Sundays there was generally a court. One of these masquerade days was for the court exclusively, and for those whom the Empress thought proper to admit; the other was for all the titled people who happened to be in the city, down to the rank of colonel, as well as those who served as officers in the guards. Sometimes, also, the whole of the nobility and the most considerable of the merchants were admitted. The court balls did not exceed 160 to 200 people; those called public received as many as 800.

When we were at Moscow, in the year 1744, the Empress took a fancy to have the court masquerades so arranged that all the men should dress as women, and all the women as men, no masks being worn. It was precisely a court day metamorphosed. The men wore large whale-boned petticoats, with women's gowns, and the head-dresses worn on court days, while the women appeared in the court costume of men. The men did not like these reversals of their sex, and the greater part of them were in the worst possible humour on these occasions, because they felt themselves to be hideous in such disguises. The women looked like scrubby little boys, whilst the more aged amongst them had thick short legs, which were anything but ornamental. The only woman who looked really well, and completely a man, was the Empress herself. As she was very tall and somewhat powerful, male attire suited her wonderfully well. She had the handsomest leg I have ever seen with any man, and her foot was admirably proportioned. She danced to perfection, and everything she did had a special grace, equally so whether she dressed as a man or as a woman. One always felt inclined to be looking at her, and turned away with regret because there was no object that could replace her.

At one of these balls I watched her while dancing a minuet. After she had ended it she came to me. I took the liberty of saying that it was very fortunate for the women she was not a man, and that her portrait alone, painted as she then was, would be enough to turn many a head. She received my compliment in very good part, and answered me in the same style, saying, in the most gracious manner possible, "That were she a man, it would be to me that she would give the apple." I stooped to kiss her hand for a compliment so unexpected. She embraced me, and every one was curious to know what had passed between us. I made no secret of it to M. Tchoglokoff, who whispered it to two or three others, and thus it passed from mouth to mouth until, in about a quarter of an hour, everybody knew it.

During the last sojourn of the court at Moscow, Prince Youssoupoff, Senator and Chief of the Corps of Cadets, had the command-in-chief of the city of St. Petersburg, where he remained during the absence of the court. For his amusement, and that of the principal persons about him, he made his cadets play alternately the best tragedies; such as the Russian ones which Soumarokoff was then composing, and the French dramas of Voltaire. These latter were spoiled. On her return from Moscow, the Empress ordered the dramas of Soumarokoff to be played at court by these young men.

She took pleasure in witnessing these representations, and it was soon noticed that she seemed to view them with more interest than could have been expected. The theatre, which was set up in one of the halls of the palace, was now transported into her own private apartments. She took pleasure in dressing up the actors, had magnificent dresses made for them, and loaded them with her jewelry. It was particularly noticed that the principal character, a rather handsome young man of eighteen or nineteen, was the most superbly dressed, as was natural.

Out of the theatre, also, he was observed to wear diamond buckles, rings, watches, very expensive lace and linen. Finally, he left the corps of cadets, and the Master of the Hounds, Count Razoumowsky, the old favourite of the Empress, immediately took him for his adjutant, which office gave him the rank of captain. The courtiers at once drew their own inferences in their usual way, and made it out that Razoumowsky, in taking Beketoff as his adjutant, could have no other motive than that of counterbalancing the favour enjoyed by M. Schouvaloff, gentleman of the bedchamber, who was known to be on no good terms with the Razoumowsky family; and, finally, it was concluded also, from the same circumstances, that this young man was coming into great favour with the Empress. It was farther known that Count Razoumowsky had placed with his new adjutant another messenger, in his service, named John Perfilievitch Yelagine, who was married to a former lady's-maid of the Empress. She it was who had furnished the young man with the linen and lace just spoken of, and, as she was anything but rich, it was easy to believe that the money for this expenditure did not come from her own purse. No one was more disturbed by the rising favour of this young man than my maid of honour, the Princess Gagarine, who was no longer young, and was anxious to make a suitable match. She had property of her own, but was not handsome; she was, however, clever and manœuvring. This was the second time she had fixed her choice on a person who afterwards attained to the favour of the Empress. The first was M. Schouvaloff; the second, this Beketoff, of whom we are speaking. There were a number of young and handsome women connected with the Princess Gagarine; and, besides, she belonged to an extensive family. All these accused M. Schouvaloff of being the secret cause of the constant reprimands which the Princess received from her Majesty on the subject of dress, and the prohibitions issued, both to her and other young ladies, against wearing—sometimes one kind of dress, and sometimes another.

In revenge for all this, the Princess and all the prettiest women of the court said everything that was bad of M. Schouvaloff, whom they all now hated, although previously he had been a great favourite. He sought to mollify them by showing them attentions, and saying pretty things to them, through his most intimate friends; but this was looked upon as an additional offence, and he was repelled and ill-received on all hands. All these ladies shunned him as they would the pestilence.

Meanwhile the Grand Duke had given me a little English barbet, which I had asked him for.

I had in my service a stove-heater, named Ivan Ouchakoff, and my people took it into their heads to name my little spaniel after this man, calling him Ivan Ivanovitch. This barbet was a most comical little creature; he walked upon his hind legs like a human being, and was in general exceedingly playful, so that we dressed him up in a different style every day, and the more he was bundled up the more playful he became. He sat at table with us, had a napkin put round him, and eat out of his plate with great propriety. Then he turned his head around and asked for drink, by yelping to the person who stood behind him. Sometimes he got upon the table to take something that suited him, such as a little pâté, a biscuit, or the like, which made the company laugh. As he was small, and incommoded no one, he was suffered to do these things, for he did not abuse the liberty allowed him, and was, too, very clean.

This barbet amused us the whole of this winter. The following summer we took him to Oranienbaum, and the Chamberlain Soltikoff, junior, having come there with his wife, both she and the other ladies of our court did nothing but sew and work for him, making all sorts of clothes and head-dresses, and disputing with each other for his possession.

At last, Madame Soltikoff got so fond of him, and the dog attached himself so much to her, that when she was going away he would not leave her, and she was as little willing to leave him. She entreated me so earnestly to allow him to go with her, that I made her a present of him. She took him under her arm, and went straight to the seat of her mother-in-law, who was then ill. This lady, seeing her arrive with the dog, and noticing the antics which she made him play, asked his name, and learning that it was Ivan Ivanovitch, she could not help expressing her astonishment in the presence of many persons, belonging to the court, who had come from Peterhoff to see her. These returned to court, and, at the end of three or four days, the whole town was filled with a marvellous story, to the effect that all the young ladies who were hostile to M. Schouvaloff, had each a white barbet, to which, in derision of the favourite of the Empress, they gave the name of Ivan Ivanovitch, and which, also, they dressed in light colours, such as Schouvaloff was fond of wearing.

Matters went so far that the Empress signified to the parents of the young ladies, that she considered it impertinent of them to permit such things. The white barbet at once changed its name, but it continued to be caressed as before, and remained in the house of the Soltikoffs, cherished by its masters till the day of its death, despite the imperial reprimand. In point of fact, the whole story was a calumny. This one dog was the only one so named, and, in giving him this name, M. Schouvaloff was not thought of. As for Madame Tchoglokoff, who did not like the Schouvaloffs, she pretended not to have noticed the name of the dog, although she was constantly hearing it, and had herself given the animal many a little pâté, while laughing at its gambols.

During the latter months of this winter, and the numerous balls and the masquerades of the court, our two former gentlemen of the bedchamber, Alexander Villebois and Zachar Czernicheff, who had been placed as colonels in the army, again made their appearance. As they were sincerely attached to me, I was very glad to see and receive them; while they, on their part, neglected no opportunity of giving me evidences of their affectionate devotion.

I was at that time very fond of dancing. At the public balls I generally changed my dress three times; my parure was very recherchée, and if the masquerade dress which I wore happened to attract general approbation, I was certain never to wear it again; for it was a rule with me that if once it produced a great effect, it could not fail to produce an inferior one on a second occasion. In the court balls, at which the public did not assist, I dressed as simply as I could, and in so doing pleased the Empress, who did not like too much display on these occasions. However, when the ladies were ordered to appear in male attire, I dressed magnificently, my clothes being richly embroidered on every seam, or otherwise in very refined taste, and this passed without criticism, nay, even pleased the Empress; why I do not very well know.

It must be confessed that at that period the efforts of coquetry were pushed to the extreme at this court; it was a constant struggle for distinction in splendour and elegance of dress. I remember, on the occasion of one of those masked balls, that every one was preparing new and most magnificent dresses, and, despairing of eclipsing others in this respect, the idea occurred to me of taking an opposite course. I put on a bodice of white gros de Tours (at that time I had a very fine shape), with a petticoat of the same, over a very small hoop. My hair, which was then very long, thick, and beautiful, was arranged behind my head, and tied with a white ribbon, en queue de renard. A single rose, with its bud and leaves, was the only ornament I wore in it; another was placed in my corset; they imitated nature so perfectly as scarcely to be distinguished from the real. Round my neck was a ruff of very white gauze, which with cuffs and an apron of the same material, completed my costume. Thus attired, I went to the ball, and the moment I entered I saw plainly that all eyes were fixed on me. I crossed the gallery without stopping, and entered the corresponding apartments beyond it.

Here I met the Empress, who instantly exclaimed, "Good God, how simple! What, not even a patch!" I laughed, and said I did not wish to add to the weight of my dress. She drew from her pocket her box of patches, and choosing one of moderate size, applied it to my face. On leaving her I hastened to the gallery, where I pointed out my patch to my more intimate friends. I did the same to the favourites of the Empress, and, as I was in high spirits, I danced more than usual. I never in my life remember to have been so highly complimented as on that occasion. I was said to be beautiful as the day—dazzlingly brilliant. I never, indeed, thought myself so very handsome, but I was pleasing; and it was in this point, I think, that my forte lay. I returned home very well satisfied with my plan of simplicity, while all the other costumes were of rare magnificence.

It was in the midst of amusements like these that the year 1750 came to a close. Madame d'Arnheim danced better than she rode; and I remember, on one occasion, that we tried which of us would be soonest tired. It turned out to be her. She was obliged to sit down, and acknowledge that she could not hold out any longer, while I still went on.

1751

AT the beginning of the year 1751 the Grand Duke, who, like myself, felt great esteem and affection for the Count de Bernis, Ambassador from the Court of Vienna, determined to consult him relative to the state of his affairs in Holstein, to the debts which burdened that country, and the negotiations opened by Denmark, to which he had consented to listen. He desired me also to mention the subject to the Count. I said I would not fail to do so, since it was his wish.

On the occasion of the next masquerade ball, therefore, I approached Count de Bernis, who was standing near the balustrade, within which the dance was going on, and told him that the Grand Duke had ordered me to speak to him respecting the affairs of Holstein. The Count listened to me with great interest and attention.

I told him frankly that being young and without advisers, having probably also but inaccurate notions of business affairs, and no experience to advance in my favour, my ideas, such as they were, were my own; that I might be very deficient in information, but that it appeared to me, in the first place, that the affairs of Holstein were not so desperate as some sought to represent them; that, besides, as to the exchange itself, I could very well understand that it might be more advantageous to Russia than to the Grand Duke personally; that assuredly, as heir to the throne, the interests of the empire ought to be dear to him; that if for these interests it was necessary to abandon Holstein in order to put an end to interminable discussions with Denmark, then the only question would be to choose, before giving it up, a favourable moment for the surrender; that to me the present time did not appear to be such, either as regarded the interest or personal credit of the Grand Duke; that, however, a time might come when circumstances would render this act more important and more creditable to him, and, perhaps, also more advantageous for the empire of Russia itself; but that at present the whole affair had a manifest air of intrigue, which, if it proved successful, would give an impression of feebleness on the part of the Grand Duke, from which he might suffer all his life in the estimation of the public; that it was but a few days, so to speak, since he had undertaken the management of that country; that he was extremely fond of the country, and yet, notwithstanding all this, he had been persuaded to exchange it, without very well knowing why, for the territory of Oldenburg, with which he was not at all acquainted, and which was still farther off from Russia; and that, besides, the port of Kiel, if in the hands of the Grand Duke, might be important for Russian navigation. The Count de Bernis entered into all my reasonings, and said, in conclusion, "As Ambassador, I have no instructions on this matter, but as Count Bernis, I think you are right." The Grand Duke told me afterwards that the Ambassador said to him, "All I can say to you in this matter is, that I think your wife is right, and that you will do well to listen to her."

The Grand Duke consequently cooled very much upon the subject, and this, probably, was noticed, for it began to be mentioned to him more rarely.

After Easter we went, as usual, for some time to the Summer Palace at Peterhoff, where, year by year, our stay became abridged. This year an occurrence took place which furnished the courtiers with matter for gossip: it was caused by the intrigues of the Messieurs Schouvaloff. Colonel Beketoff, of whom I have spoken above, not knowing what to do with himself during the favour which he enjoyed, although it increased to such a point that, from day to day, people were waiting to see which of the two would yield his place to the other, that is to say, Beketoff to John Schouvaloff, or the latter to Beketoff—not knowing, as I have said, how to amuse himself, it occurred to him to have the Empress' choir of singing boys perform at his own residence. In several of them he took a special interest, on account of the beauty of their voices; and as both himself and his friend Yelagine were versifiers, they composed songs which the children sung.

To this an odious interpretation was given; for it was well known that nothing was more detested by the Empress than vice of such a nature. Beketoff, in the innocence of his heart, would walk in the garden with these children; this was imputed to him as a crime. The Empress went away to Zarskoe-Selo for a couple of days, and then returned to Peterhoff, where M. Beketoff received orders to remain, under the plea of indisposition. He did, in fact, remain there with Yelagine, caught there a violent fever, which threatened his life, and in the ravings of his delirium, did nothing but talk about the Empress, with whom he was thoroughly taken up. He recovered; but he remained in disgrace, and retired, after which he was placed in the army, where he was not successful. He was too effeminate for the profession of arms.

In the meanwhile we proceeded to Oranienbaum, where we went hunting every day. Towards autumn, in the month of September, we returned to the city. The Empress placed at our court M. Leon Narichkine as gentleman of the bedchamber. He immediately hastened from Moscow with his mother, his brother, his brother's wife, and his three sisters.

He was one of the most singular persons I have ever known, and no one has ever made me laugh so much as he has done. He was a born harlequin, and had he not been by birth what he was, he might have gained a subsistence, and a handsome one too, by his extraordinary talent for humour. He was not at all wanting in understanding. He had heard of everything, and everything arranged itself in his head after a fashion of his own. He could give a dissertation on any art or science he chose. He would employ all the technical terms belonging to his subject, and would talk to you for a quarter of an hour or more without stopping; and at the end, neither himself nor any one else would understand anything of the string of words which had flowed so readily from his lips, and the whole, of course, would finish with a general burst of laughter. Among other things he said of history, that he did not like history in which there were histories, and that in order that a history should be good it must be devoid of history, that otherwise history became mere rant.

But it was on politics that he was inimitable. When he began on this subject, it was impossible for any one, however serious, to resist him. He used to say, too, that of well-written plays the greater part were very wearisome.

Scarcely had he been appointed to the court when the Empress sent orders to his eldest sister to marry a M. Seniavine, who, for that purpose, was placed in our court as gentleman of the bedchamber. This was a thunderbolt for the young lady, who consented to this marriage with the greatest repugnance. It was very ill received by the public also, and all the blame of it was cast on M. Schouvaloff, the favourite of the Empress, who, before his rise to favour, had been very partial to this young lady, for whom they made up this bad match in order that he might lose sight of her.

This was a species of persecution truly tyrannical. At last she married, became consumptive, and died.

By the end of September, we returned to the Winter Palace. The court was at this time so badly off for furniture that the same mirrors, beds, chairs, tables, and drawers which served us at the Winter Palace, passed with us to the Summer Palace, and thence to Peterhoff, following us even to Moscow.

A good number were broken and cracked in these different journeys, and, in this state of dilapidation, they were supplied to us; so that it was difficult to make use of them, while to get others an express order from the Empress was required.

As she was almost always very difficult of access, if not inaccessible, I resolved to buy, by degrees, with my own money, chests of drawers and the other more necessary articles of furniture, as well for the Winter as the Summer Palace; so that when I passed from the one house to the other, I found everything I wanted without difficulty and without the inconveniences of transport. The Grand Duke was pleased with this arrangement, and he made a similar one in his own apartments. As for Oranienbaum, which belonged to the Grand Duke, we had, at my cost, everything we needed in my private apartments. I procured all this at my own expense in order to avoid all dispute and difficulty; for his Imperial Highness, although very lavish where his own fancies were concerned, was not at all so in anything that regarded me; and generally he was anything but liberal. But as all I did in my own apartments and with my own purse served to embellish his house, he was quite content with it.

During this summer Madame Tchoglokoff conceived such a special and real affection for me, that on our return to the capital she could not do without me, and was quite ennuyée when I was not with her. The cause of this affection arose from my not responding to the advances which it had pleased her husband to make to me—a circumstance which gave me a peculiar merit in the eyes of his wife. When we returned to the Winter Palace, Madame Tchoglokoff invited me almost every evening to her rooms. There were not many people there, but always more than in my room, where I sat quite alone reading, except when the Grand Duke came in to walk up and down at a rapid pace, talking about things which interested himself, but which had no value in my eyes. These promenades would last one or two hours, and were repeated several times a-day. I was obliged to walk with him till my strength was quite exhausted, to listen with attention, and to answer him, though, for the most part, what he said had neither head nor tail; for he often gave the reins to his imagination. I remember that, during one whole winter, he was taken up with a project of building, near to Oranienbaum, a pleasure-house in the form of a convent of Capuchins, where he and I and all his suite should be dressed as Capuchins. This dress he thought charming and convenient. Every one was to have a donkey, and, in his turn, take this donkey and fetch water and bring provisions to the so-called convent. He used to laugh till he was ready to drop at the idea of the admirable and amusing effects which this invention was to produce. He made me draw a pencil-sketch of the plan of this precious work, and every day I had to add or remove something. However determined I was to comply with his humours, and bear everything with patience, I frankly avow that I was very often worn out with the annoyance of these visits, promenades, and conversations, which were insipid beyond anything I have ever seen. When he was gone, the most tiresome book appeared a delightful amusement.

Towards the end of autumn, the balls for the court and the public recommenced, as did also the rage for splendour and refinement in masquerade dresses. Count Zachar Czernicheff returned to St. Petersburg. As, on the ground of old acquaintance, I always treated him very well, it rested only with myself to give what interpretation I pleased to his attentions this time. He began by telling me that I had grown much handsomer. It was the first time in my life that anything of the kind had been said to me. I did not take it ill. Nay, more; I was credulous enough to believe that he spoke the truth. At every ball there was some fresh remark of this kind. One day, the Princess Gagarine brought me a device from him, and, on breaking it, I perceived that it had been opened and gummed together again. The motto, as usual, was printed, but it consisted of a couple of verses, very tender and full of sentiment. After dinner, I had some devices brought to me. I looked for a motto which might serve as an answer, without compromising myself. I found one, put it into a device representing an orange, and gave it to the Princess Gagarine, who delivered it to Count Czernicheff. Next morning she brought me another from him; but this time I found a motto of some lines, in his own hand. I answered it, and there we were in regular and quite sentimental correspondence. At the next masquerade, while dancing with him, he said he had a thousand things to tell me which he could not trust to paper, nor put in a device, which the Princess Gagarine might break in her pocket or lose on the way; and he entreated me to grant him a moment's audience either in my chamber, or wherever I might deem suitable. I told him that that was an utter impossibility, that my rooms were inaccessible, and that it was also impossible for me to leave them. He told me that he would, if necessary, disguise himself as a servant; but I refused point-blank, and so the matter went no farther than this secret correspondence by means of devices. At last the Princess Gagarine began to suspect its character, scolded me for making use of her, and would not receive any more of these missives.

1752

Amid these occurrences the year 1751 came to a close, and 1752 began. At the end of the Carnival, Count Czernicheff left to join his regiment. A few days before his departure I required to be bled; it was on a Saturday. The following Wednesday, M. Tchoglokoff invited me to his island, at the mouth of the Neva. He had a house there, consisting of a saloon in the centre and some chambers on the sides. Near this house he had some slides prepared. On arriving, I found there the Count Roman Voronzoff, who, on seeing me, said, "I have just the thing for you; I have had an excellent little sledge made for the slides." As he had often taken me before, I accepted his offer, and the sledge was at once brought.

In it was a kind of small fauteuil, on which I seated myself. He placed himself behind me, and we began to descend; but about half-way down the incline, the Count was no longer master of the sledge, and it overturned. I fell, and the Count, who was heavy and clumsy, fell on me, or rather on my left arm, in which I had been bled some four or five days before. We got up, and walked towards one of the court sledges, which was in waiting for those who descended to convey them back to the point from which they had started, so that any who wished might recommence the descent. While sitting in this sledge with the Princess Gagarine, who, with Prince Ivan Czernicheff, had followed me, the latter, together with Voronzoff, standing behind the sleigh, I felt a sensation of warmth spreading over my left arm, the cause of which I could not make out. I passed my right hand into the sleeve of my pelisse to see what was the matter, and having withdrawn it, I found it covered with blood. I told the Counts and the Princess that I thought my vein had reopened.

They made the sleigh move faster, and instead of going again to the slides, we went to the house. There we found no one but a butler. I took off my pelisse, the butler gave me some vinegar, and Count Czernicheff performed the office of surgeon. We all agreed not to say a word about this adventure.

As soon as my arm was set to rights, we returned to the slides. I danced the rest of the evening, then supped, and we returned home very late, without any one having the least idea of what had happened to me. However, the skin did not join smoothly for nearly a month; but it got all right by degrees.

During Lent I had a violent altercation with Madame Tchoglokoff, the cause of which was as follows: My mother had been for some time in Paris. The eldest son of General Ivan Fedorovitch Gleboff, upon his return from that capital, brought me, from her, two pieces of very rich and very beautiful stuff. While looking at them in my dressing-room, in the presence of Skourine, who unfolded them, I chanced to say that they were so beautiful that I felt tempted to present them to the Empress; and I really was watching an opportunity of speaking of them to her Majesty, whom I saw but very rarely, and then, too, mostly in public. I said nothing about them to Madame Tchoglokoff. It was a present I reserved for myself to make. I forbade Skourine to mention to any one what had fallen from my lips in his hearing. Skourine, however, went instantly to Madame Tchoglokoff, and told her what I had said. A few days afterwards, Madame Tchoglokoff came into my room and told me that the Empress sent me her thanks for my stuffs; that she had kept one of them and returned the other. I was thunderstruck on hearing this. I said to her, "How is this, Madame Tchoglokoff?"

Upon this she stated that she had carried the stuffs to the Empress, having heard that I intended them for her Majesty. For the moment I felt vexed beyond measure, more so indeed than I ever remember to have been before. I stammered; I could scarcely speak. However, I said that I had proposed to myself a treat in presenting these things to the Empress myself, and that she had deprived me of this pleasure by carrying them off without my knowledge, and presenting them in that fashion to her Imperial Majesty; I reminded her that she could not know my intentions, as I had never spoken of them to her, or that if she was aware of them, it was only from the mouth of a treacherous servant, who had betrayed his mistress, who daily loaded him with kindness. Madame Tchoglokoff, who always had reasons of her own, replied, and maintained that I ought never speak to the Empress myself about anything; that she had signified to me the order of her Imperial Majesty to this effect, and that my servants were in duty bound to report to her all that I said; that, consequently, Skourine had only done his duty, and she hers, in carrying, without my knowledge, to her Majesty the stuffs I had destined for her, and that the whole matter was quite in rule. I let her speak on, for rage stopped my utterance. At last she went away. I then entered a small ante-chamber, where Skourine generally remained in the morning, and where my clothes were kept, and seeing him there, I gave him, with all my force, a well-aimed and heavy box on the ear.

I told him he was a traitor, and the most ungrateful of men, for having dared to repeat to Madame Tchoglokoff what I had forbidden him to speak about; that I had loaded him with kindnesses, while he betrayed me even in such innocent words; that from that day forward I would never give him anything more, but would get him dismissed and well beaten. I asked him what he expected to gain by such conduct, telling him that I should always remain what I was, while the Tchoglokoffs, hated and detested by every one, would, in the end, get themselves dismissed by the Empress herself, who most assuredly would sooner or later discover their intense stupidity, and utter unfitness for the position in which the intrigues of a wicked man had placed them; that, if he chose, he might go and repeat to them all I had said; that he could not injure me by so doing, while he would soon see what would become of himself. The man fell at my feet crying bitterly, and begged my pardon with a repentance which appeared to me sincere. I was touched by it, and told him that his future conduct would show me what course I must take with him, and that by his behaviour I would regulate my own. He was an intelligent fellow, by no means deficient in character, and one who never broke his word to me.

On the contrary, I have had the best proofs of his zeal and fidelity in the most difficult times. I complained to every one

I could of the trick Madame Tchoglokoff had played me, in order that the matter might reach the Empress' ears. The Empress, when she saw me, thanked me for my present, and I learned from a third party, that she disapproved of the way in which Madame Tchoglokoff had acted. And thus the matter ended.

After Easter we went to the Summer Palace. I had observed for some time that the Chamberlain, Serge Soltikoff, was more assiduous than usual in his attendance at court. He always came there in company with Leon Narichkine, who amused every one by his originality, of which I have already reported several traits. Serge Soltikoff was the aversion of the Princess Gagarine, of whom I was very fond, and in whom I even reposed confidence. Leon Narichkine was looked upon as a person of no sort of consequence, but very original. Soltikoff insinuated himself as much as possible into the good graces of the Tchoglokoffs. As these people were neither amiable, nor clever, nor amusing, he must have had some secret object in these attentions. Madame Tchoglokoff was at this time pregnant, and frequently indisposed.

As she pretended that I amused her during the summer quite as much as in the winter, she often requested me to visit her. Soltikoff, Leon Narichkine, the Princess Gagarine, and some others, were generally at her apartments, whenever there was not a concert at the Grand Duke's, or theatricals at court. The concerts were very wearisome to M. Tchoglokoff, who always assisted at them; but Soltikoff discovered a singular mode of keeping him occupied. I cannot conceive how he contrived to excite in a man so dull, and so utterly devoid of talent and imagination, a passion for versifying and composing songs which had not even common sense. But having made this discovery, whenever anyone wished to get rid of M. Tchoglokoff, it was only necessary to ask him to make a new song. Then, with much empressement, he would go and sit down in a corner of the room, generally near the stove, and set to work upon his song—a business which took up the evening. The song would be pronounced charming, and thus he was continually encouraged to make new ones.

Leon Narichkine used to set them to music, and sing them with him; and while all this was going on, we conversed without restraint. I once had a large book of these songs, but I know not what has become of it.

During one of these concerts, Serge Soltikoff gave me to understand what was the object of his assiduous attentions. I did not reply to him at first. When he again returned to the subject, I asked him what it was he wanted of me? Hereupon he drew a charming and passionate picture of the happiness which he promised himself. I said to him, "But your wife, whom you married for love only two years ago, and of whom you were supposed to be passionately fond—and she, too, of you— what will she say to this?"

He replied that all was not gold that glitters, and that he was paying dearly for a moment of infatuation. I did all I could to make him change his mind—I really expected to succeed in this—I pitied him. Unfortunately, I listened also. He was very handsome, and certainly had not his equal at the Imperial court, still less at ours. He was not wanting in mind, nor in that finish of accomplishments, manner, and style which the great world gives, and especially a court. He was twenty-six years old.

Take him all in all, he was by birth, and by many other qualities, a distinguished gentleman. As for his faults, he managed to hide them. The greatest of all was a love of

Yekaterina Vorontsova-Dashkova, the closest female friend of Empress Catherine and a major figure of the Russian Enlightenment

intrigue and a want of principle. These were not unfolded to my eyes. I held out all the spring, and a part of the autumn. I saw him almost every day, and made no change in my conduct towards him. I was the same to him as I was to all others, and never saw him but in the presence of the court, or of a part of it. One day, to get rid of him, I made up my mind to tell him that he was misdirecting his attentions. I added, "How do you know that my heart is not engaged elsewhere?"

This, however, instead of discouraging him, only made his pursuit all the more ardent. In all this there was no thought of the dear husband, for it was a known and admitted fact, that he was not at all amiable, even to the objects with whom he was in love; and he was always in love; in fact, he might be said to pay court to every woman, except the one who bore the name of his wife; she alone was excluded from all share of his attentions.

In the midst of all this, Tchoglokoff invited us to a hunting party on his island, whither we went in a skiff, our horses being sent on before. Immediately on our arrival I mounted my horse, and we went to find the dogs. Soltikoff seized the moment when the rest were in pursuit of the hares to approach me and speak of his favourite subject.

I listened more attentively than usual. He described to me the plan which he had arranged for enshrouding, as he said, in profound mystery, the happiness which might be enjoyed in such a case. I did not say a word. He took advantage of my silence to persuade me that he loved me passionately, and he begged that I would allow him to hope, at least, that he was not wholly indifferent to me. I told him he might amuse himself with hoping what he pleased, as I could not prevent his thoughts. Finally he drew comparisons between himself and others at the court, and made me confess that he was preferable to them. From that he concluded that he was preferred. I laughed at all this, but I admitted that he was agreeable to me. At the end of an hour and a-half's conversation, I desired him to leave me, since so long a conversation might give rise to suspicion. He said he would not go unless I told him that I consented. I answered, "Yes, yes; but go away." He said, "Then it is settled," and put spurs to his horse. I cried after him, "No, no;" but he repeated, "Yes, yes."

And thus we separated. On our return to the house, which was on the island, we had supper, during which there sprung up such a heavy gale from the sea, that the waves rose so high that they even reached the steps of the house.

In fact, the whole island was under water to the depth of several feet. We were obliged to remain until the storm had abated, and the waters retreated, which was not until between two and three in the morning. During this time, Soltikoff told me that heaven itself had favoured him that day, by enabling him to enjoy my presence for a longer time, with many other things to the same effect. He thought himself already quite happy. As for me, I was not at all so.

A thousand apprehensions troubled me, and I was unusually dull, and very much out of conceit with myself. I had persuaded myself that I could easily govern both his passions and my own, and I found that both tasks were difficult, if not impossible.

Two days after this, Soltikoff informed me that one of the Grand Duke's valets de chambre, Bressan, a Frenchman, had told him that his Imperial Highness had said in his room, "Sergius Soltikoff and my wife deceive Tchoglokoff, make him believe whatever they like, and then laugh at him." To tell the truth, there was something of this kind, and the Grand Duke had perceived it. I answered, by advising him to be more circumspect for the future. Some days afterwards I caught a very bad sore throat, which lasted more than three weeks, with a violent fever, during which the Empress sent to me the Princess Kourakine, who was about to be married to Prince Lobanoff. I was to dress her hair. For this purpose she had to sit on my bed, in her court-dress and hooped petticoats. I did my best; but Madame Tchoglokoff, seeing that it was impossible for me to manage it, made her get off my bed, and finished dressing her herself. I have never seen the lady since then.

The Grand Duke was at this period making love to Mademoiselle Martha Isaevna Schafiroff, whom the Empress had recently placed with me, as also her elder sister, Anna Isaevna. Serge Soltikoff, who was a devil for intrigue, insinuated himself into the favour of these girls, in order to learn anything the Grand Duke might say to them relative to him.

These young ladies were poor, rather silly, and very selfish, and, in fact, they became wonderfully confidential in a very short time. In the midst of all this we went to Oranienbaum, where again I was every day on horseback, and wore no other than a man's dress, except on Sundays. Tchoglokoff and his wife had become as gentle as lambs.

In the eyes of Madame Tchoglokoff I possessed a new merit; I fondled and caressed a great deal one of her children, who was with her. I made clothes for him, and gave him all sorts of playthings and dresses. Now the mother was dotingly fond of this child, who subsequently became such a scapegrace that, for his pranks, he was sentenced to confinement in a fortress for fifteen years. Soltikoff had become the friend, the confidant and the counsellor of M. and Madame Tchoglokoff. Assuredly no person in his senses could ever have submitted to so hard a task as that of listening to two proud, arrogant, and conceited fools, talking nonsense all day long, without having some great object in view. Many, therefore, were the guesses, many the suppositions, as to what this object could be. These reached Peterhoff and the ears of the Empress. Now at this period it often happened that when her Majesty wished to scold any one, she did not scold for what she might well complain of, but seized some pretext for finding fault about something which no one would ever have thought she could object to. This is the remark of a courtier; I have it from the lips of its author, Zachar Czernicheff. At Oranienbaum, every one of our suite had agreed, men as well as women, to have, for this summer, dresses of the same colour; the body gray, the rest blue, with a collar of black velvet, and no trimmings.

This uniformity was convenient in more respects than one. It was on this style of dress that she fixed, and more especially on the circumstance that I always wore a riding habit, and rode like a man at Peterhoff. One court day the Empress said to Madame Tchoglokoff that this fashion of riding prevented my having children, and that my dress was not at all becoming; that when she rode on horseback she changed her dress. Madame Tchoglokoff replied, that as to having children, this had nothing to do with the matter; that children could not come without a cause; and that, although their Imperial Highnesses had been married ever since 1745, the cause nevertheless did not exist.

Thereupon her Imperial Majesty scolded Madame Tchoglokoff, and told her she blamed her for this, because she neglected to lecture, on this matter, the parties concerned; and on the whole, she showed much ill-humour, and said that her husband was a mere night-cap, who allowed himself to be worn by a set of dirty-nosed brats (des morveux).

All this, in four-and-twenty hours, had reached their confidants. At this term of morveux, the morveux wiped their noses; and, in a very special council held on the matter by them, it was resolved and decreed that, in order to follow out strictly the wishes of her Imperial Majesty, Sergius Soltikoff and Leon Narichkine should incur a pretended disgrace at the hands of M. Tchoglokoff, of which perhaps he himself would not be at all aware; that under pretext of the illness of their relatives, they should retire to their homes for three weeks or a month, in order to allow the rumours which were current to die away. This was carried out to the letter, and the next day they departed, to confine themselves to their own houses for a month. As for me, I immediately changed my style of dress; besides, the other had now become useless. The first idea of this uniformity of attire had been suggested to us by the dress worn on court-days at Peterhoff.

The body was white, the rest green, and the whole trimmed all over with silver lace. Soltikoff, who was of a dark complexion, used to say that he looked like a fly in milk, in this dress of white and silver. I continued to frequent the society of the Tchoglokoffs as before, although it was now dreadfully wearisome. The husband and wife were full of regrets for the absence of the chief attractions of their society, in which most assuredly I did not contradict them.

The illness of Soltikoff prolonged his absence, and during it the Empress sent us orders to come from Oranienbaum and join her at Cronstadt, whither she was about to proceed, in order to admit the waters into the canal of Peter I.

That Emperor had commenced the work, and just then it was completed. She arrived at Cronstadt before us.

The night following was very stormy, and, as immediately on her arrival, she had sent us orders to join her, she supposed we must have been caught in the storm, and was in great anxiety all night. She fancied that a ship, which could be seen from her window, labouring in the sea, might be the yacht in which we were to make the voyage. She had recourse to the relics which she always kept by her bedside; carried them to the window, and kept moving them in a direction opposite to the ship which was tossing in the storm. She exclaimed repeatedly that we should certainly be lost, and that it would be all her fault, because a short time previously she had sent us a reprimand for not showing her more prompt obedience, and she now supposed we must have set out immediately on the arrival of the yacht. But, in fact, the yacht did not reach Oranienbaum until after the storm, so that we did not go on board until the afternoon of the next day.

We remained three days at Cronstadt, during which the blessing of the canal took place with very great solemnity, and the waters were, for the first time, let into it. After dinner there was a grand ball. The Empress wished to remain at Cronstadt to see the waters let out again, but she left on the third day without this having been effected. The canal was never dried from that time, until, in my reign, I caused the steam-mill to be constructed which empties it. Otherwise, the thing would have been impossible, the bottom of the canal being lower than the sea; but this was not perceived at that time.

From Cronstadt every one returned to his own quarters; the Empress went to Peterhoff, and we to Oranienbaum. M. Tchoglokoff asked and obtained leave to go for a month to one of his estates. During his absence Madame Tchoglokoff gave herself a great deal of trouble to execute the Empress' orders to the letter. At first she had many conferences with Bressan, the Grand Duke's valet de chambre. Bressan found at Oranienbaum a pretty woman named Madame Groot, the widow of a painter. It took several days to persuade her, to promise her I know not what, and then to instruct her in what they wanted of her, and to what she was to lend herself. At last Bressan was charged with the duty of making this young and pretty widow known to the Grand Duke. I clearly saw that Madame Tchoglokoff was deep in some intrigue, but I knew not what. At last, Serge Soltikoff returned from his voluntary exile, and told me pretty nearly how matters stood. Finally, after much trouble, Madame Tchoglokoff gained her end, and when she felt sure of this she informed the Empress that everything was going on as she wished. She expected a great reward for her trouble; but in this she was much mistaken, for nothing was given her; however, she maintained that the Empire was in her debt. Immediately after this we returned to the city.

It was at this time that I persuaded the Grand Duke to break off the negotiations with Denmark. I reminded him of the advice of the Count de Bernis, who had already departed for Vienna. He listened to me, and ordered the negotiations to be closed without anything being concluded: and this was done. After a short stay at the Summer Palace, we returned to the Winter Palace.

It seemed to me that Serge Soltikoff was beginning to be relax in his attentions; that he became absent, sometimes absurd, arrogant, and dissipated. I was vexed at this, and spoke to him on the subject. He gave me but poor excuses, and pretended that I did not understand the extreme cleverness of his conduct. He was right, for I did think it strange enough. We were told to get ready for the journey to Moscow, which we did. We left St. Petersburg on the 14th of December, 1752. Soltikoff remained behind, and did not follow us for several weeks after. I left the city with some slight indications of pregnancy. We travelled very rapidly day and night. At the last stage before reaching Moscow, these signs disappeared with violent spasms. On our arrival, and seeing the turn things were taking, I felt satisfied that I had had a miscarriage. Madame Tchoglokoff also remained behind at St. Petersburg, as she had just been delivered of her last child, which was a girl. This was the seventh. On her recovery she joined us at Moscow.

1753

Here we lodged in a wing built of wood, constructed only this autumn, and in such a way that the water ran down the wainscoting, and all the apartments were exceedingly damp. This wing consisted of two ranges of apartments, each having five or six large rooms, of which those looking to the street were for me, and those on the other side for the Grand Duke. In the one intended for my toilet, my maids and ladies of the bedchamber were lodged, together with their servants; so that there were seventeen girls and women lodged in one room, which had, it is true, three large windows, but no other outlet than my bed-room, through which, for every kind of purpose, they were obliged to pass, a thing neither pleasant for them nor for me. We were obliged to put up with this inconvenience, of which I have never seen the like. Besides, the room in which they took their meals was one of my ante-chambers. I was ill when I arrived.

To remedy this inconvenience, I had some very large screens placed in my bed-room, by means of which I divided it into three; but this was scarcely of any use, for the doors were opening and shutting continually, as was unavoidable. At last, on the tenth day, the Empress came to see me, and observing the continual passing to and fro, she went into the other chamber, and said to my women, "I will have a different outlet made for you than through the sleeping-room of the Grand Duchess." But what did she do? She ordered a partition to be made, which took away one of the windows of a room in which, even before this, seventeen persons could hardly exist. Here, then, was the chamber made smaller in order to gain a passage; the window was opened towards the street, a flight of steps was led up to it, and thus my women were obliged to pass and repass along the street. Under their window, necessaries were placed for them; in going to dinner, they must again pass along the street. In a word, this arrangement was worthless, and I cannot tell how it was that these seventeen women, thus huddled up and crowded together, did not catch a putrid fever; and all this, too, close to my bed-room, which, in consequence, was so filled with vermin of every kind that I could not sleep.

At last, Madame Tchoglokoff, having recovered after her accouchement, arrived at Moscow, as did, some days later, Serge Soltikoff. As Moscow is very large, and people much dispersed in it, he availed himself of this locality, so favourable to the purpose, to conceal the decrease of his attentions, feigned or real, at court. To tell the truth, I was grieved at this; however, he gave me such good and specious reasons for it, that as soon as I had seen him and spoken to him, my annoyance on the subject vanished. We agreed that, in order to decrease the number of his enemies, I should get some remark repeated to Count Bestoujeff which might lead him to hope that I was less averse to him than in former days. With this message I charged a person called Bremse, who was employed in the Holstein Chancery of M. Pechline.

This person, when not at court, frequently went to the residence of the Chancellor Count Bestoujeff. He eagerly accepted the commission, and brought me back word that the Chancellor was delighted, and said that I might command him as often as I thought proper, and that if, on his part, he could be of any use to me, he begged me to point out to him some safe channel by which we might communicate with each other. I perceived his drift, and I told Bremse that I would think of it. I repeated this to Soltikoff, and it was immediately settled that he should go to the Chancellor on the plea of a visit, as he had but just arrived. The old man gave him a most cordial reception; took him aside, spoke to him of the internal condition of our court, of the stupidity of the Tchoglokoffs, saying, among other things, "I know, although you are their intimate friends, that you understand them as well as I do, for you are a young man of sense." Then he spoke of me, and of my situation, just as if he had lived in my room; adding, "In gratitude for the good-will which the Grand Duchess has so kindly evinced for me, I am going to do her a little service, for which she will, I think, thank me.

I will make Madame Vladislava as gentle as a lamb for her, so that she will be able to do with her whatever she pleases; she will see that I am not such an ogre as I have been represented to her." Finally, Serge Soltikoff returned, enchanted with his commission and his man. He gave him some advice for himself, also, as wise as it was useful. All this made him very intimate with us, without any one having the least suspicion of the fact.

In the meanwhile Madame Tchoglokoff, who never lost sight of her favourite project of watching over the succession, took me aside one day and said, "Listen to me, I must speak to you with all sincerity." I opened my eyes and ears, and not without cause. She began with a long preamble, after her fashion, respecting her attachment to her husband, her own prudent conduct, what was necessary and what was not necessary for ensuring mutual love and facilitating conjugal ties; and then she went on to say, that occasionally there were situations in which a higher interest demanded an exception to the rule. I let her talk on without interruption, not knowing what she was driving at, a good deal astonished, and uncertain whether it was not a snare she was laying for me, or whether she was speaking with sincerity.

Just as I was making these reflections in my own mind, she said to me, "You shall presently see whether I love my country, and whether I am sincere; I do not doubt but you have cast an eye of preference upon some one or other; I leave you to choose between Sergius Soltikoff and Leon Narichkine—if I do not mistake, it is the latter." Here I exclaimed, "No no! not at all." "Well, then," she said, "if it be not Narichkine, it is Soltikoff." To that I made no reply, and she went on saying, "You shall see that it will not be I who will throw difficulties in your way." I played the simpleton to such a degree, that she scolded me for it several times, both in town and in the country, whither we went after Easter.

It was at that time, or thereabout, that the Empress gave to the Grand Duke the lands of Liberitza, and several others, at a distance of fourteen or fifteen verstes from Moscow. But before we went to reside on these new possessions of his Imperial Highness, the Empress celebrated the anniversary of her coronation at Moscow. This was the 25th of April.

It was announced to us that she had ordered the ceremony to be observed exactly as it had been on the very day of her coronation. We were curious to know how this would be. The evening before, she went to sleep at the Kremlin.

We stayed at the Sloboda, in the wooden palace, and received orders to go to mass at the cathedral. At nine o'clock in the morning we started from the wooden palace in the state carriage, our servants walking on foot. We traversed the whole of Moscow, step by step—the distance through the city being as much as seven verstes—and we alighted at the cathedral. A few moments after the Empress arrived with her retinue, wearing the small crown on her head, and the imperial mantle, borne as usual by her chamberlains. She went to her ordinary seat in the church, and in all this there was, as yet, nothing unusual—nothing that was not practised at all the other fêtes of her reign. The church was damp and cold to a degree that I had never before felt. I was quite blue, and frozen in my court-dress and with bare neck.

The Empress sent me word to put on a sable tippet, but I had not one with me. She ordered her own to be brought, took one, and put it on her neck. I saw another in the box, and thought she was going to send it to me, but I was mistaken— she sent it back. This I thought a pretty evident sign of displeasure. Madame Tchoglokoff, who saw that I was shivering, procured me, from some one, a silk kerchief, which I put round my neck. When mass and the sermon were over, the Empress left the church, and we were preparing to follow her, when she sent us word that we might return home.

It was then we learned that she was going to dine alone on the throne, and that in this respect the ceremonial would be observed just as it was on the day of her coronation, when she had dined alone. Excluded from this dinner, we returned, as we had come, in great state, our people on foot, making a journey of fourteen verstes, going and returning, through the city of Moscow, and we benumbed with cold and dying of hunger. If the Empress seemed to us in a very bad temper during mass, this disagreeable evidence of want of attention, to say no more, did not leave us in the best of humours either. At the other great festivals, when she dined on the throne, we had the honour of dining with her; this time she repelled us publicly. Returning alone in the carriage with the Grand Duke, I told him what I thought of this, and he said that he would complain of it. On reaching home, half dead with cold and fatigue, I complained to Madame Tchoglokoff of having caught cold. The next day there was a ball at the wooden palace; I said I was ill, and did not go.

This image of Catherine and Peter shortly after their marriage, encapsulates Peter and Catherine's relationship perfectly.

The Grand Duke really did make some complaint or other to the Schouvaloffs on the subject, and they sent him some answer, which appeared satisfactory to him, and nothing more was said about the matter.

About this time we learned that Zachar Czernicheff and Colonel Nicholas Leontieff had had a quarrel, while at play, in the house of Roman Voronzoff; that they had fought with swords, and that Zachar Czernicheff had received a severe wound in the head. It was so serious that he could not be removed from Count Voronzoff's house to his own.

He remained there, was very ill, and there was some talk of trepanning him. I was very sorry for him, for I liked him very much. Leontieff was arrested by order of the Empress. This combat set the whole city in a ferment, on account of the extensive connections of both the champions. Leontieff was the son-in-law of the Countess Roumianzoff, a very near relative of the Panines and Kourakines. The other, also, had relatives, friends, and protectors. The occurrence had taken place at the house of Count Roman Voronzoff; the wounded man was still there. At last, when the danger was over, the affair was hushed up, and matters went no farther.

In the course of the month of May, I again had indications of pregnancy. We went to Liberitza, an estate of the Grand Duke, twelve or fourteen verstes from Moscow. The stone house which was on it, had been built a long time ago by Prince Menchikoff, and was now falling to decay, so that we could not live in it. As a substitute, tents were set up in the court, and every morning, at two or three o'clock, my sleep was broken by the sound of the axe, and the noises made in building a wooden wing, which was being hurriedly erected, within two paces, so to speak, of our tents, in order that we might have a place to live in during the remainder of the summer. The rest of our time we spent in hunting, walking, or riding. I no longer went on horseback, but in a cabriolet. About the Feast of St. Peter we returned to Moscow.

I was seized with such drowsiness that I slept every day till noon, and then it was only with difficulty that I was awakened in time for dinner. The Feast of St. Peter was kept in the usual way: I was present at Mass, at the dinner, the ball, and the supper. Next morning I felt great pains in my loins. Madame Tchoglokoff summoned a midwife, who predicted the miscarriage, which actually occurred the following night. I might have been with child two or three months.

For thirteen days I was in great danger, as it was suspected that a portion of the after-birth had remained behind.

This circumstance was kept a secret from me. At last, on the thirteenth day, it came away of itself—without pain, or even a struggle. In consequence of this accident I had to keep my room for six weeks, during which the heat was insupportable. The Empress came to see me the day I fell ill, and appeared to be affected by my state. During the six weeks that I kept my room I was nearly tired to death. The only society I had was Madame Tchoglokoff, who came but rarely, and a little Kalmuck girl, whom I liked for her pretty, agreeable ways. I frequently cried from ennui. As for the Grand Duke, he was mostly in his own room, where one of his valets, a Ukrainian, named Karnovitch, a fool as well as a drunkard, did his best to amuse him; furnishing him with toys, with wine, and such other strong liquors as he could procure, without the knowledge of M. Tchoglokoff, who, in fact, was deceived and made a fool of by every one. But in these nocturnal and secret orgies with the servants of the chamber, among whom were several young Kalmucks, the Grand Duke often found himself ill-obeyed and ill-served; for, being drunk, they knew not what they did, and forgot that they were with their master, and that that master was the Grand Duke. Then his Imperial Highness would have recourse to blows with his stick, or the blade of his sword; but in spite of all this, he was ill-obeyed; and more than once he had recourse to me, complaining of his people, and begging me to make them listen to reason. On these occasions I used to go to his rooms, give them a good scolding, and remind them of their duties, when they would instantly resume their proper places.

This made the Grand Duke often say to me, and also to Bressan, that he could not conceive how I managed those people; for, as for himself, though he belaboured them soundly, yet he could not make them obedient, while I, with a single word, could get them to do whatever I wished. One day when I went for this purpose into the apartments of his Imperial Highness, I beheld a great rat, which he had had hung—with all the paraphernalia of an execution—in the middle of a cabinet, formed by means of a partition. I asked him what all this meant. He told me that this rat had committed a crime; one which, according to the laws of war, was deserving of capital punishment; it had climbed over the ramparts of a fortress of cardboard which he had on the table in his cabinet, and had eaten two sentinels, made of pith, who were on duty at the bastions. He had had the criminal tried by martial law, his setter having caught him, and he was immediately hung, as I saw, and was to remain there exposed to the public gaze for three days, as an example.

I could not help bursting into a loud laugh at the extreme folly of the thing; but this greatly displeased him. Seeing the importance he attached to the matter, I retired, excusing myself on account of my ignorance, as a woman, of military law; but this did not prevent his being very much out of humour with me on account of my laughter. In justification of the rat, however, it may at least be said, that he was hung without having been questioned or heard in his own defence.

During this stay of the court at Moscow, it happened that one of the court footmen became insane, and violently so. The Empress gave orders that her chief physician, Boërhave, should take charge of him. He was placed in a chamber close to that of Boërhave, who resided at court. Besides this case, it also happened that several other persons went out of their mind this year. In proportion as these cases came under the notice of the Empress, she had the persons brought to court and lodged near Boërhave, so that they formed a sort of mad-house at court. I remember that the principal persons among them was Tchedajeff, a major of the Semenofsky guards; a Lieutenant-Colonel Lintrum; a Major Tchoglokoff; a monk of the convent of Voskresensky, who emasculated himself with a razor, and several others. The madness of Tchedajeff consisted in his believing Nadir-Schah, otherwise Thamas-Kuli-Khan, the usurper and tyrant of Persia, to be God. When the physicians could not succeed in curing him of his delusion, they placed him in the hands of the priests. These persuaded the Empress to have him exorcised. She herself assisted at the ceremony; but Tchedajeff remained, to all appearance, as mad as before. There were, however, people who had doubts of his lunacy, as he was quite reasonable on every other point, but that of Nadir-Schah; his friends even consulted him about their affairs, and he gave them very sensible advice. Those who did not believe him mad, gave as a reason for his affectation of madness his having had some trouble on his hands, from which he extricated himself by this ruse. At the beginning of the Empress' reign he had been supervisor of taxes, had been accused of extortion, and was threatened with a trial, in dread of which he took up this fancy, which extricated him from the difficulty.

In the middle of August, 1753, we returned to the country. To keep the 5th of September, the Feast of the Empress, she went to the convent of Voskresensky. Whilst there, the church was struck with lightning; fortunately her Imperial Majesty was in a chapel at the side of the great church, and only learnt the fact through the terror of the courtiers; however, there was no one either hurt or killed by the accident. A little while afterwards she returned to Moscow, whither we also repaired from Liberitza. Upon our return to the city, we saw the Princess of Courland kiss the Empress' hand in public for the permission which had been given her to marry Prince George Hovansky. She had quarrelled with the object of her first engagement, Peter Soltikoff, who immediately afterwards married a Princess Sonzoff.

On the 1st of November of this year, at three o'clock in the afternoon, I was in Madame Tchoglokoff's room, when her husband, Serge Soltikoff, Leon Narichkine, and several other gentlemen of the court, left us to go to the apartments of the Chamberlain Schouvaloff, to congratulate him on his birthday, which fell on that day. Madame Tchoglokoff, the Princess Gagarine, and I were talking together, when, after hearing some noise in a little chapel close by, a couple of these gentlemen ran in, telling us that they had been prevented from passing through the halls of the chateau, as it was on fire. I immediately went to my room, and, as I passed through an ante-chamber, I saw that the balustrade at the corner of the great hall was on fire. It was about twenty paces from our wing. On entering my apartments, I found them already filled with soldiers and servants, who were removing the furniture, and carrying off everything they could. Madame Tchoglokoff followed me, and as there was nothing more to be done but wait till it caught fire, we left.

At the gate we found the carriage of the chapel-master, Araga, who had come to attend a concert given by the Grand Duke, whom I had already informed of the accident. We entered the carriage: the streets were covered with mud, in consequence of the previous heavy rains. Here we had a view of the fire and of the way in which the people were carrying out the furniture from every part of the house. I here saw a strange sight, viz: the astonishing number of rats and mice which were descending the staircase in file without over-much hurrying themselves. The want of engines rendered it impossible to save this immense wooden structure, and, besides, the few that were there were kept under the very staircase which was on fire; this, too, occupied very nearly the centre of the surrounding buildings, which covered a space of some two or three verstes in circumference. The heat became so great that we could not bear it, so that we were obliged to have the carriage driven some few hundred paces outwards. At last M. Tchoglokoff and the Grand Duke came and told us that the Empress was going to Pokrovsky House, and had given orders that we should go to M. Tchoglokoff's, which formed the right hand corner of the main street of the Sloboda. We at once repaired thither. The house had a hall in the centre and four chambers on each side. It was hardly possible to be more uncomfortable than we were here; the wind blew in every direction, the windows and doors were all half rotten, and the planks of the floor open to the breadth of three or four inches; besides this, there was vermin everywhere. Here resided the children and servants of M. Tchoglokoff. As we entered they were sent out, and we were lodged in this horrible house, which was almost bare of furniture.

On the day after we took up our abode here, I saw what a Kalmuck's nose could hold. The little girl whom I kept near me, on my waking, pointed to her nose, and said, "I have a nut here." I felt her nose, but could not find anything. All the morning, however, she kept repeating, over and over again, that she had a nut in her nose. She was a child of from four to five years old. No one could tell what she meant by a nut in her nose. But about noon, as she was running along, she fell down, and struck against the table. This made her cry; while crying, she took out her pocket-handkerchief and wiped her nose, and in doing so the nut fell from it. I saw this myself, and could then understand how a nut, which could not be held in any European nose without being perceived, might be held in the hollow of a Kalmuck nose, which is placed within the head between two immense cheeks.

Our clothes, and everything else, had been left in the mud in front of the burning palace, and were brought to us during the night and following day. What I most regretted was my books. I was at this time just finishing the fourth volume of Bayle's Dictionary: I had spent two years in reading it, and got through a volume every six months. From this one may judge of the solitude in which my life was passed. At last my books were brought to me. My clothes were found, those of the Countess Schouvaloff, etc. Madame Vladislava showed me, as a curiosity, this lady's petticoats. They were lined behind with leather, as she was unable to retain her water—an infirmity which had afflicted her ever since her first accouchement. All her petticoats were impregnated with the smell, and I sent them back in all haste to the owner.

In this fire the Empress lost all that had been brought to Moscow of her immense wardrobe. She did me the honour of telling me that she had lost 4,000 dresses, and that of all these the only one that she regretted was the one made from the piece of stuff which I had received from my mother. She also lost, on this occasion, several other valuables; amongst them a bowl covered with engraved stones, which Count Roumianzoff had purchased at Constantinople, and for which he had paid 8,000 ducats. All those effects had been placed in a wardrobe over the hall which had caught fire.

This hall served as a vestibule to the grand hall of the palace. At ten o'clock in the morning, the men whose duty it was to light the stoves had come to heat this entrance-hall. After putting the wood into the stove, they lighted it as usual.

This done, the room became filled with smoke; they thought that it escaped by some imperceptible holes in the stove, and set to work to cover with clay the interstices of the tiles. The smoke increasing, they tried to find some chinks in the stove, but not finding any, they perceived that the outlet must be between the partitions of the apartment.

These partitions were only of wood. They got water, and put out the fire in the stove, but the smoke still increased, and made its way into the ante-chamber, where there was a sentinel of the horse-guards. The latter, expecting to be suffocated, and not daring to move from his post, broke a pane of glass, and began to cry out; but no one coming to his assistance, nor hearing him, he fired his musket through the window. The report was heard by the main guard, which was posted opposite the palace. They ran to him, and on coming in, found the place filled with a dense smoke, out of which they withdrew the sentinel. The stove heaters were put under arrest. They had hoped to extinguish the fire, or at least prevent the smoke from increasing without being obliged to give any alarm; and they had been hard at work with this view for five hours.

This fire gave rise to a discovery on the part of M. Tchoglokoff. The Grand Duke had in his apartments several very large chests of drawers. As they were being carried out, some of the drawers, being either open or badly fastened, disclosed to the spectators what they were filled with. Who would have thought it? The drawers contained nothing but a great quantity of bottles of wine and strong liquors. They served his Imperial Highness for a cellar. Tchoglokoff spoke to me on the matter, and I told him I was quite ignorant of the circumstance, which was the truth; I knew nothing of it, but I was a frequent, indeed, almost a daily witness of the Grand Duke's drunkenness.

After the fire we remained in Tchoglokoff's house for nearly six weeks. While residing here, we often had to pass in front of a house, situated in a garden near the Soltikoff Bridge. It belonged to the Empress, and was called the Bishop's House, because she had bought it of a bishop. The idea occurred to us of asking her Majesty, unknown to the Tchoglokoffs, to allow us to occupy it, for it appeared to us, and we were also told that it was, more habitable than the one we were in.

We received orders to go and take up our abode in the Bishop's House. It was a very old wooden house, from which there was no view, but it was built on stone vaults, and by this means was higher than the one we had just quitted, which had only a ground floor. The stoves were so old, that when lighted, one could see the fire through the furnace, so numerous were the chinks and cracks, while the rooms were filled with smoke. We all had headaches and sore eyes. In fact, we ran the risk of being burnt alive in this house. There was only one wooden staircase, and the windows were very high.

The place actually did catch fire two or three times while we were there, but we succeeded in extinguishing the flames.

I caught there a bad sore throat, with a great deal of fever. The day I fell ill, M. de Breithardt, who had returned to Russia on the part of the Austrian court, was to sup with us, previously to taking leave. He found me with red and swollen eyes, and thought I had been crying: nor was he mistaken: ennui, indisposition, and the physical and moral discomforts of my position had given me much hypochondria. During the whole day, which I passed with Madame Tchoglokoff, waiting for those who never came, she kept saying every moment, "See how they desert us." Her husband had dined out, and taken everybody with him. In spite of all the promises which Serge Soltikoff had made us to steal away from this dinner party, he only returned with M. Tchoglokoff. All this put me in a very bad humour. At last, some days afterwards, we were allowed to go to Liberitza. Here we thought ourselves in paradise; the house was quite new, and tolerably well fitted up. We danced every evening, and all our court was collected there. At one of these balls we saw the Grand Duke occupied a long while in whispering to M. Tchoglokoff, who, subsequently, appeared vexed, absent, and more close and scowling than usual. Serge Soltikoff seeing this, and finding that Tchoglokoff treated him with great coolness, went and sat down by the side of Mademoiselle Martha Schafiroff, and tried to discover what could be the meaning of this unusual intimacy between the Grand Duke and M. Tchoglokoff. She told him that she did not know, but that the Grand Duke had on several occasions said to her, "Serge Soltikoff and my wife deceive Tchoglokoff in the most unheard-of way.

He is in love with the Grand Duchess; but she cannot endure him: Soltikoff is the confidant of Tchoglokoff, and makes him believe that he is working for him with my wife, while instead of that he is working for himself with her.

She can very well endure Soltikoff, for he is amusing: she makes use of him to manage Tchoglokoff just as she pleases, and, in reality, she laughs at them both. I must undeceive that poor devil Tchoglokoff, who excites my pity. I must tell him the truth, and then he will see who is his true friend—my wife or I." As soon as Soltikoff became aware of this dangerous dialogue, and of his delicate position in consequence, he repeated it to me, and then went and seated himself by the side of Tchoglokoff, and asked him what was the matter with him. The latter at first was unwilling to enter into any explanation, and merely sighed; then he began uttering jeremiads on the difficulty of finding faithful friends.

At last Soltikoff turned and twisted him in so many different directions, that he drew from him an avowal of the conversation which he had just had with the Grand Duke. No one certainly could have formed any idea of what had passed between them, without being told of it. The Grand Duke began by making great protestations of friendship to Tchoglokoff, saying that it was only in the most important circumstances of life that it was possible to distinguish true friends from false; that to show the sincerity of his own friendship, he was going to give him a very emphatic proof of his frankness; that he knew, beyond doubt, that he was in love with me; that he did not impute it to him as a crime that I should appear agreeable to him, for that no one was master of his own heart; but that, nevertheless, he ought to apprise him that he had made a bad choice of confidants, and in his simplicity believed Serge Soltikoff to be his friend,

and working in his interest with me, whereas he was only working for himself, and he suspected he was his rival; that, as for me, I laughed at them both, but if M. Tchoglokoff would follow his advice and trust in him then he would see that he was his only and true friend. M. Tchoglokoff gave the Grand Duke many thanks for his friendship, and his proffers of friendship; but in reality he considered all the rest as mere chimeras and delusions on his part.

It may easily be believed that, in any case, he did not much wish for a confidant who, both by his rank and character, was as little to be trusted as he was able to be useful. This matter being once stated, Soltikoff had but little trouble in restoring tranquillity to Tchoglokoff's mind, for he was not in the habit of attaching much importance nor paying much attention to the discourses of a person so devoid of judgment, and so generally known to be so. When I learnt all this, I must confess I was extremely indignant with the Grand Duke, and, to prevent his returning to the subject, I told him that I was not ignorant of what had passed between him and Tchoglokoff. He blushed, said nothing, went off, sulked, and so the matter ended.

On returning to Moscow, we left the Bishop's House for apartments in what was called the Empress' Summer House, which had not been burnt. The Empress had had new apartments constructed in the space of six weeks. For this purpose beams had been transported from Perova House, from Count Hendrikoff's, and from the dwelling of the Princes of Georgia. At last she took possession of these rooms about the beginning of the new year.

1754

The Empress kept the new-year's day of 1754 in this palace, and the Grand Duke and I had the honour of dining with her in public on the throne. At table, her majesty seemed very lively and talkative. Around the throne, tables were laid for several hundred persons of the highest rank. At dinner the Empress asked who was that thin and ugly woman, with a crane's neck, whom she saw seated there (pointing to the place); she was told it was Mademoiselle Martha Schafiroff. She burst into a laugh, and, turning to me, remarked that this reminded her of a Russian proverb, which said, "A long neck is only good for hanging." I could not but smile at the point of this imperial sarcasm, which did not fall unheeded, for the courtiers passed it on from mouth to mouth, so that on rising from table, I found several persons who already knew of it. Whether the Grand Duke heard it, I know not, but at all events he did not allude to it, and I took care not to mention it to him.

Never was a year more fertile in fires than that of 1753-54. I have several times seen, from the windows of my apartments in the Summer Palace, two, three, four, and even five fires at once in different parts of Moscow. During the Carnival, the Empress gave orders for several balls and masquerades to be given in her apartments, at one of which I saw her engaged in a long conversation with the wife of General Matiouchkine. This lady was unwilling that her son should marry the Princess Gagarine. But the Empress persuaded her, and the Princess Gagarine, who numbered a good thirty years, had permission to marry M. Dmitri Matiouchkine. She was much pleased at this, and so was I. It was a marriage of inclination. Matiouchkine was at this time very handsome. Madame Tchoglokoff did not come with us to our summer apartments. Under different pretexts she remained, with her children, in her own house, which was very near the court. But the truth is, that, virtuous and loving wife as she was, she had conceived a passion for Prince Peter Repnine, and a marked aversion for her husband. She thought she could not be happy without a confidant, and I appeared to her the most trustworthy person. She showed me all the letters she received from her lover. I kept her secret faithfully, with scrupulous exactitude and prudence. Her interviews with the Prince were very secret; yet in spite of this the husband had some suspicions.

An officer of the horse-guards named Kaminine, had given rise to them. This man was jealousy and suspicion personified: it was his nature. He was an old friend of Tchoglokoff. The latter opened his mind to Serge Soltikoff, who endeavoured to tranquillize him. I was careful not to tell Soltikoff anything I knew, for fear of some involuntary indiscretion on his part. At last the husband also sounded me a little. I pretended ignorance and astonishment, and held my tongue.

In the month of February I had some signs of pregnancy. On Easter Sunday, during mass, Tchoglokoff fell ill of the dry cholic; they gave him various remedies, but his disease only grew worse. During Easter week, the Grand Duke, with the gentlemen of our court, went out riding. Serge Soltikoff was of the number. I remained at home, for they were afraid to let me go out in my present condition, especially as I had twice miscarried. I was alone in my room when M. Tchoglokoff sent me a request to come to him. I went, and found him in bed. He made a thousand complaints of his wife; told me she saw Prince Repnine; that he went to her house on foot; that, during the Carnival, he had gone there, one courtball day, dressed as a harlequin; that Kaminine had had him followed; in short, God only knows all the details he gave me.

Just as he was most excited, his wife arrived; whereupon he began, in my presence, to load her with reproaches, telling her that she deserted him in his sickness. They were both very suspicious and narrow-minded. I was nearly frightened to death lest his wife should suspect that it was I who had betrayed her, from the mass of details which he then went into relative to her interviews. His wife, on the other hand, told him that it was not strange if she punished him for his conduct towards her; that neither he, nor any one else, could reproach her with having ever until now failed in her duty towards him in any respect; and she ended with saying that it ill became him to complain. Both appealed continually to me as a witness of what they said. I held my tongue, fearing to offend the one or the other, or compromise myself: my face was burning from apprehension. I was alone with them. When the quarrel was at its highest, Madame Vladislava came in to tell me that the Empress had just entered my room. I ran back immediately. Madame Tchoglokoff left at the same time, but, instead of following me, she stopped in a corridor, where there was a staircase leading into the garden, and there, as I was afterwards told, she sat down. As for myself, I reached my room quite out of breath, and found the Empress there. As she saw that I was out of breath and rather red, she asked where I had been. I told her that I was just come from the apartments of M. Tchoglokoff, who was ill, and that I had run in order to get back as quickly as possible, having been informed that she had condescended to come to my rooms. She did not ask me any more questions, but seemed to me to be dwelling upon what I had said, as if it appeared strange to her. Nevertheless, she continued speaking to me. She did not ask where the Grand Duke was, for she knew he had gone out. Neither he nor I, during the whole of her reign, dared to go out in the city or leave the house, without first sending to ask her permission. Madame Vladislava was in the room: the Empress addressed her several times, then spoke to me, and always of indifferent matters: finally, after a visit of nearly half an hour, she went away, saying that, in consequence of my pregnancy, she would dispense with my appearing on the 21st and 25th of April. I was surprised that Madame Tchoglokoff had not followed.

When the Empress had gone, I asked Madame Vladislava what had become of her. She informed me that she had sat down on the stairs, and burst into tears. Upon the return of the Grand Duke, I recounted to Serge Soltikoff what had occurred during their absence; how Tchoglokoff had sent for me; my alarm at what had been said between the husband and wife, and the visit which the Empress had paid me. His answer was: "If that be the case, I am of opinion that the

Empress must have come to see what you do in the absence of your husband; and, in order that it may be seen that you are perfectly alone, both in your own apartments and in those of the Tchoglokoffs, I will be off, and take all my comrades to the house of Ivan Schouvaloff, just as we are, bespattered with mud up to our eyes." And, in fact, when the Grand Duke retired, he went off with all those who had been riding with his Imperial Highness to Ivan Schouvaloff, who had apartments at the court. When they arrived there, Schouvaloff asked them questions about their ride, and Soltikoff told me afterwards that, from these questions, it seemed to him that he had been correct in his inference.

From this day the illness of Tchoglokoff grew worse and worse. On the 21st of April—my birth-day—the physicians pronounced him beyond hope of recovery. The Empress was informed of this, and gave orders (as she was accustomed to do) that he should be carried to his own house, in order that he might not die at court, for she was afraid of the dead. I was very much grieved on learning his condition. He died at the very time when, after many years of trouble and pain, we had succeeded in rendering him not only less ill-natured and mischievous, but even tractable, and when, by dint of studying his character, we had acquired the power of managing him as we pleased. As for his wife, she at this time loved me sincerely, and, from a harsh and spiteful Argus, had become a firm and attached friend. Tchoglokoff, after his removal to his own house, lived until the afternoon of the 25th of April, the day of the Empress' coronation, when he died.

I was immediately informed of the event, as I kept constantly sending to his house. I was truly sorry for him, and wept a good deal. His wife, too, was confined to her bed during the last days of her husband's illness; he was at one side of the house, she in the other. Serge Soltikoff and Leon Narichkine happened to be in her room at the moment of her husband's death; the windows being open, a bird flew into the room, and alighted on the cornice of the ceiling, right opposite to Madame Tchoglokoff's bed. Upon seeing this, she said, "I am certain that my husband has just breathed his last; send and ask how he is." She was informed that he was really dead. She said that that bird was the soul of her husband. They tried to prove to her that the bird was an ordinary bird; but then it could not be found. They said it had flown away, but as no one had seen it, she remained convinced that it was the soul of her husband who had come to find her.

As soon as the funeral was over, Madame Tchoglokoff wished to come to my rooms. The Empress seeing her passing along the Yaousa bridge, sent her word that she would dispense with her attendance on me, and that she might return to her own house. Her Imperial Majesty took it ill that, as a widow, she should have gone out so soon. The same day she named M. Alexander Ivanovitch Schouvaloff to discharge the duties of the late M. Tchoglokoff in the Grand Duke's court.

Now this M. Schouvaloff, not so much on his own account as from the place he held, was the terror of the court, the city, and the whole empire. He was the chief of the tribunal of the state inquisition, which was then called the Secret Chancery. His functions, it was said, had given him a sort of convulsive movement, which seized the whole of the right side of his face from the eye to the jaw, whenever he was affected either with joy, anger, fear, or anxiety. It was astonishing that such a man, with so hideous a grimace, should ever have been chosen for a post which placed him continually in the presence of a pregnant young woman. Had I been delivered of an infant having that same wretched twitch, I think the Empress would have been greatly vexed, and this might have happened, seeing him as I did constantly, never with my own wish, and, for the greater part of the time, with a shudder of involuntary repugnance, on account of his personal appearance, his connections, and his office, by which, as may easily be imagined, the pleasure of his society was not likely to be augmented. But this was only a beginning of the "good times" they were preparing for us, and especially for me. The next morning I was informed that the Empress was going to place with me again the Countess Roumianzoff.

I knew that she was the sworn enemy of Serge Soltikoff, that she bore no love to the Princess Gagarine, and that she had greatly injured my mother in the estimation of the Empress. The moment I became aware of this arrangement, I lost all patience. I wept bitterly, and told Count Schouvaloff that if the Countess Roumianzoff was placed with me I should look upon it as a great misfortune; that this lady had already injured my mother, had blackened her in the eyes of the Empress, and that now she would do the same with me; that she was feared as a pest when she was formerly in our suite, and that there would be many rendered miserable by the arrangement if he could not find means to prevent it. He promised to do what he could, and tried to tranquillize me. As, in my situation, he dreaded the effect of such excitement, he went at once to the Empress, and on his return told me that he hoped the Countess Roumianzoff would not be placed about my person. And, in fact, I heard no more of the matter, and nothing was now thought of but our departure for St. Petersburg. It was settled that we should be twenty-nine days on the road; that is to say, that we should only travel one post-station each day. I was frightened to death lest Serge Soltikoff and Leon Narichkine should be left behind at Moscow; but I know not how it was, they had the condescension to inscribe their names in the list of our suite.

At last, on the 10th, or the 11th, we set out from the palace of Moscow. I was in a carriage with the wife of Count

Alexander Schouvaloff, the most tiresome woman that it is possible to imagine. Madame Vladislava, and the midwife, whom, as I was pregnant, they said I could not do without, were with us. I was tired to death in that carriage, and did nothing but cry. At last, the Princess Gagarine, who personally disliked the Countess Schouvaloff, because her daughter, who was married to Golofkine, a cousin of the Princess, made herself disagreeable to the relatives of her husband, seized a moment when she could get near me to say that she was working hard to make Madame Vladislava favourable to me, as she feared, as did every one else, that the hypochondria which my condition produced might do me harm, as well as injure my child. Soltikoff, she said, dared not come near me, because of the restraint and constant presence of the Schouvaloffs, both husband and wife. She did, in fact, succeed in getting Madame Vladislava to listen to reason, and condescend so far as to mitigate a little the state of perpetual annoyance and restraint which gave rise to this hypochondria which I found it impossible to control. All I wanted was the merest trifle—only a few moments of conversation. At last she succeeded. After this tedious journey of twenty-nine days, we reached St. Petersburg and the Summer Palace. The Grand Duke at once re-established his concerts. This gave me sometimes the opportunity of a little conversation; but my hypochondria had become such that at every moment, and at every word, my eyes filled with tears, and my mind was disturbed with apprehensions; in a word, I could not get it out of my head that everything tended to the removal of Serge Soltikoff.

We went to Peterhoff. I walked a great deal, but in spite of this my melancholy followed me. In the month of August we returned to the city, to occupy again the Summer Palace. It was a death-blow to me when I learned that, for my accouchement, they were preparing apartments close to, and forming part of those belonging to the Empress.

Alexander Schouvaloff took me to see them; I found two rooms, gloomy, and with only one issue, like all those of the Summer Palace; the hangings were of ugly crimson damask, there was scarcely any furniture, and no kind of convenience. I saw that I should be isolated there, without any sort of company, and thoroughly wretched. I said so to Soltikoff and to the Princess Gagarine, who, though they bore no love to each other, had nevertheless a point of union in their friendship for me. They saw the matter as I did, but it was impossible to remedy it. I was to go on the Wednesday to these apartments, which were far removed from those of the Grand Duke. I went to bed on Tuesday evening, and in the night awoke with labour-pains. I called Madame Vladislava, who went to fetch the midwife. She pronounced that I was in labour. The Grand Duke, who was sleeping in his own room, was awakened, as also Count Alexander Schouvaloff.

The latter sent word to the Empress, who was not long in coming. It was about two o'clock in the morning. I was very ill. At last, towards noon the next day, the 20th September, I gave birth to a son. As soon as it was dressed the Empress called in her confessor, who gave the child the name of Paul, after which the Empress immediately bade the midwife take the child up and follow her. I remained on the bed on which I had been confined. Now this bed was placed opposite a door through which I could see the light; behind me were two large windows which did not close properly, and on the right and left of this bed were two doors, one of which opened into my dressing-room, and the other into the room in which Madame Vladislava slept. As soon as the Empress left, the Grand Duke also went away, as likewise did M. and Madame Schouvaloff, and I saw no one again until three o'clock in the afternoon. I had perspired a great deal, and begged Madame Vladislava to change my linen, and put me into my own bed, but she told me that she dared not. She sent several times to call the midwife, who, however, did not come. I asked for something to drink, but still received the same answer.

At last, after three hours, the Countess Schouvaloff arrived, very elaborately dressed. When she saw me lying just where she had left me, she was very angry, and said it was enough to kill me. This was very consolatory, certainly.

I had been in tears from the time of my delivery, pained by the neglect in which I was left, after a severe labour; uncomfortably accommodated, lying between doors and windows, which did not shut close, no one daring to lift me into my bed, which was not two paces off, and to which I had not the strength to crawl. Madame Schouvaloff departed immediately, and went, I think, to fetch the midwife; for the latter came in about half an hour afterwards, and told us that the Empress was so taken up with the child that she would not let her go away for a moment. As for me no one gave me a thought. This forgetfulness or neglect was not at all flattering. I was dying of thirst. At last they placed me on my bed, and I did not see a living soul for the rest of the day, nor did any one send even to ask after me.

The Grand Duke, for his part, did nothing but drink with all he could find, and the Empress was taken up with the child. In the city and throughout the empire the joy at this event was great. The next day I began to feel an excruciating rheumatic pain, from the hip down the thigh and left leg. This pain prevented me from sleeping, and this brought on a violent fever. In spite of all this, the attentions I received next day were just of the same character. I saw no one, and no one inquired after me. The Grand Duke, indeed, did come into my room for a moment, and then went away, saying, that he had not time to stop. I did nothing but weep and moan in my bed. Nobody was in my room but Madame Vladislava;

Burney. Russian empress winter travelling

in her heart she was sorry for me, but she had not the power to remedy this state of things. Besides, I never liked to be pitied nor to complain. I had too proud a spirit for that, and the very idea of being unhappy, was insupportable to me. Hitherto I had done whatever I could not to appear so. I might have seen Count Alexander Schouvaloff and his wife, but they were such insipid and tiresome people that I was always delighted when they were not present. On the third day a messenger came from the Empress to Madame Vladislava to ask if a blue satin mantelet which her Imperial Majesty had worn on the day of my accouchement, had been left in my room. Madame Vladislava searched for it everywhere in my rooms, and it was at last found in a corner of my dressing-room, where it had not been noticed, as, since my confinement, that room had seldom been entered. Having found it, she sent it off immediately. This mantelet, as we afterwards learned, gave rise to a somewhat singular occurrence. The Empress had no fixed hours either for going to bed or getting up, for dinner, supper nor dressing. On one of those three days she was lying, after dinner on a sofa on which she had placed a mattress and pillows. While there, feeling cold, she asked for this mantelet. It was sought for everywhere, but could not be found, as it had been left in my room. The Empress then ordered that it should be looked for under the pillows of her bed, believing that it would be found there. The sister of Madame Krause, the Empress' favourite lady's maid, passed her hand under the bolster of her Majesty's bed and drew it back, saying, that there was no mantle there, but there was a packet of hair there, or something like it, she did not know what. The Empress immediately rose from her place, and had the mattress and the pillows taken up, and under them was found, to their no small astonishment, a paper in which was some hair twisted round the roots of some herbs. Upon this her Majesty's maids, and the Empress herself, said that assuredly it was some charm or witchcraft, and every one began guessing who it could be that had the hardihood to place the packet under the Empress' pillow. Suspicion lighted on one of those most in the favour of her Imperial Majesty. She was known by the name of Anna Dmitrevna Doumacheva. Not long since she had become a widow, and had married a second time a valet de chambre in the service of the Empress. The Schouvaloffs did not like this woman, who was in their way, as well by the esteem in which she was held as by the confidence reposed in her by the Empress ever since her youth. She was quite capable of playing them some trick which might diminish their influence. As they were not without their partisans, these began to view the matter in a criminal light; to this view the Empress was of herself sufficiently disposed, since she believed in charms and sorcery. Consequently, she gave orders to Count Alexander Schouvaloff to have the woman arrested, together with her husband and her two sons, one of whom was an officer of the guards, and the other a page of the chamber to her Majesty. Her husband, two days after his arrest, asked for a razor to shave with, and cut his throat with it. As for the wife and her two children, they were a long time under arrest, and she confessed that, with a view to prolong the Empress' favour, she had made use of charms, and had on Holy Thursday put some grains of burnt salt into a glass of Hungarian wine, which she had presented to the Empress. The affair was concluded by banishing the woman and her two sons to Moscow. A rumour was afterwards set afloat that a fainting fit, which the Empress had a little time before my accouchement, was caused by the drink which this woman had given to her. It is certain, however, that she never gave her more than two or three grains of burnt salt, which most assuredly could never have hurt her. In all this there was nothing reprehensible, but the woman's rashness and superstition.

At last the Grand Duke, growing weary of his evenings passed without my ladies of honour, came and proposed to spend an evening in my room. At this time he was courting the very ugliest of these ladies, Elizabeth Voronzoff. On the sixth day my son's baptism took place. He had already come near dying of the thrush. It was only by stealth that I could get any account of him; for to have inquired about him would have passed for a doubt of the Empress' care, and would have been very ill received. Besides, she had taken him into her own room, and whenever he cried she herself would run to him, and, through excess of care, they were literally stifling him. He was kept in a room extremely warm, wrapped up in flannel, and laid in a cradle, lined with black fox furs; over him was a coverlet of quilted satin, lined with wadding, and above this one of rose-coloured velvet, lined with black fox skins. I saw him myself, many times afterwards, lying in this style, the perspiration running from his face and whole body, and hence it was that, when older, the least breath of air that reached him chilled him and made him ill. Besides, he had in attendance on him a great number of aged matrons who, by their ill-judged cares, and their want of common sense, did him infinitely more harm than good, both physically and morally. On the day of his baptism, after the ceremony, the Empress came into my room, and brought me, on a golden salver, an order on her cabinet for 100,000 roubles. She had added to it a small casket, which I did not open until she was gone.

 This money came very seasonably, for I had not a sous, and was heavily in debt. As for the casket, when I opened it, I was not greatly dazzled; it contained only a very poor necklace, with ear-rings and two wretched rings, such as I should have been ashamed to give to my maids. In the whole case there was not a jewel worth 100 roubles; neither was the taste nor workmanship any better. I said nothing, but locked up the imperial casket. It would seem that the meanness of the present was felt, for Count Alexander Schouvaloff was ordered to inquire how I liked the jewel-case.

I replied, that whatever came from the hands of the Empress was always of inestimable value in my eyes. With that compliment he went away apparently well pleased. He returned to the charge when he saw that I never wore this beautiful necklace, and especially those miserable ear-rings, telling me to put them on. I said that on the Empress' fêtes I was accustomed to wear the most beautiful things I possessed, and that this necklace and ear-rings did not come within that category.

Four or five days after the money ordered by the Empress was brought to me, Baron Tcherkassoff, her secretary of the cabinet, sent to beg of me, for Heaven's sake, to lend it again to the cabinet, because the Empress had asked for money, and there was not a sou left. I sent it back to him, and he repaid me in the month of January. The Grand Duke having heard of the present made me by the Empress, got into a terrible passion because nothing had been given to him.

He complained vehemently to Count Alexander Schouvaloff. The latter told the Empress, who immediately sent the Duke an order for a similar sum, and it was to meet this demand that my money was borrowed. The truth is, the Schouvaloffs were very timid, and it was by this weakness that they were to be led; but this trait had not then been discovered.

After my son's baptism, there were fêtes, balls, illuminations, and fireworks at court. As for me, I was all the while in bed, ill, and suffering dreadfully from ennui. At last they chose the seventeenth day after my confinement to announce to me two pieces of agreeable news at once. First of all, that Serge Soltikoff had been selected to carry the news of the birth of my son to Sweden; secondly, that the marriage of the Princess Gagarine was fixed for the following week; that is to say, in plain language, that I was about to be deprived, almost immediately, of the two persons I most liked of all who were about me. I buried myself more than ever in my bed, where I did nothing but grieve. In order to be able to keep to it, I pretended an increase of the pains in my thigh, which prevented my getting up; but the truth was, I neither could nor would see anybody, I felt so miserable.

During my confinement, the Grand Duke had also a great affliction, for he learned from Count Alexander Schouvaloff, that one of his old huntsmen, named Bastien, whom the Empress a few years before had ordered to marry Mademoiselle Schenck, my old lady's-maid, had come to give information of his having heard, from some one or other, that Bressan wished to give something or other to the Duke to drink. Now this Bastien was a great scoundrel and drunkard, who from time to time used to drink with his Imperial Highness, and having quarrelled with Bressan, whom he supposed to stand higher in the Duke's favour than himself, thought to do him an ill turn. The Duke was fond of them both. Bastien was sent to the fortress; Bressan expected to be sent there also, but escaped with nothing worse than the fright. The huntsman was banished the country, and sent to Holstein with his wife, while Bressan retained his place because he served as a general spy. Serge Soltikoff, after some delays, occasioned by the usual dilatoriness of the Empress in signing papers, at last took his departure. The Princess Gagarine, in the meanwhile, was married at the time fixed.

When the forty days of my confinement were over, the Empress, on occasion of the churching, came a second time into my chamber. I had risen from my bed to receive her, but she saw that I was so weak and exhausted, that she made me sit down during the prayers which were read by her confessor. My child was brought into the room; it was the first time I had seen him since his birth. I thought him very pretty, and the sight of him raised my spirits a little; but the moment the prayers were finished, the Empress had him carried away, and then left me. The 1st of November was fixed by her Majesty for my receiving the customary felicitations after the six weeks of my confinement. For this purpose, the room next to mine was magnificently fitted up, and there, seated on a couch of rose-colored velvet, embroidered with silver, everyone came to kiss my hand. The Empress came also, and from my apartments she went to the Winter Palace, and we received orders to follow her two or three days after. We were lodged in the apartments formerly occupied by my mother, and which properly formed a part of Yagoujisky House, and half of Ragousinsky House; the other half being occupied by the Department of Foreign Affairs. The Winter Palace was at this time in course of erection near the great Square.

I passed from the Summer to the Winter Palace, with the firm resolution of not quitting my room as long as I did not feel myself strong enough to conquer my hypochondria. I read at this period the history of Germany, and the Universal History of Voltaire. After these I read, during this winter, as many Russian works as I could procure; among others two immense volumes of Baronius, translated into Russian; next I lit upon the Esprit des Lois of Montesquieu, after which I read the annals of Tacitus, which caused a singular revolution in my brain, to which, perhaps, the melancholy cast of my thoughts at this period contributed not a little. I began to take gloomier views of things, and to look for more hidden and interested motives in the occurrences around me. I gathered all my strength in order to be able to go out at Christmas, and, in fact, I was present at divine service; but while at church I was seized with a shivering and with pains all over my body, so that upon my return home I undressed and went to bed, my bed being merely a pallet, which I had placed before a blocked-up door, through which it seemed to me that no draughts could come, as in addition to a curtain lined with woollen cloth, there was also before it a large screen; but yet I believe it was the cause of all the colds which afflicted me this winter. The day after Christmas, the violence of the fever was so great that I became delirious. When I shut my eyes I saw nothing but the ill-drawn figures of the tiles of the stove, which was at the foot of my pallet, the room being small and narrow. As to my bed-room, I never went into it at all, for it was very cold, as the windows, on two sides, looked out upon the Neva, towards the east and north. A second reason which banished me from it, was the proximity of the Grand Duke's apartments, where all day long, and for a part of the night, there was a noise and racket just like that of a guard-house. Besides this, as he and all his associates smoked a great deal, the disagreeable smoke and smell of tobacco was perceptible there. I remained, therefore, all the winter in this poor little narrow chamber, which had two windows and a pier between them, so that, in all, the area may have been seven or eight archines in length, by four in breadth, with three doors.

(Continue on the third volume)

РИСУНКИ

ОДЕЖДЫ и ВООРУЖЕНІЯ

РОССІЙСКИХЪ

ВОЙСКЪ.

PLATES LIST OF ILLUSTRATIONS

656. Private and Trumpeter light legged regiments, from 1786 to 1796

657. Officer of the light-colored regiments, from 1786 to 1796

658. Officer of light-legged regiments in the army of prince Potemkin, from 1788 to 1792

659. A horse farmer in 1788

660. Horse Yegorsky Officer in 1788

661. Officer from 1789 to 1792 and Private from 1789 to 1796

662. Horse Yegorsky drummer, from 1790 to 1796

663. Horse Yegorsky Officer from 1792 to 1796

664. General mayor and general adjutant field cavalry, from 1764 to 1780

665. Cavalry's generals, from 1780 to 1796

666. Drummer and musketeers battalions of the St. Petersburg legion, from 1765 to 1775

667. NCO and Officer of the St. Petersburg legion, from 1769 to 1775

668. High Officer of the St. Petersburg legion, from 1765 to 1775

669. Grenadier and a jager of the St. Petersburg legion, from 1769 to 1775

670. Grenadiers shapki Petersburg and Moscow legions, from 1769 to 1775

671. Carabiner of the St. Petersburg legion, from 1769 to 1775

672. Officer and NCO carabinier squadrons of the St. Petersburg legion, from 1769 to 1775

673. Private and NCO hussars squadrons of the st. Petersburg legion from 1765 to 1775

674. Hussar Officer of the St. Petersburg legion, from 1765 to 1775

675. NCO of the St. Petersburg legion, from 1769 to 1775

676. Cossack Officer of the St. Petersburg legion, from 1765 to 1775

677. Men of artillery, engineering. NCO and the ober-quartermaster of the St. Petersburg legion, from 1769 to 1775

678. Jaeger and musketeer of the Moscow legion, from 1769 to 1775

679. Grenadiers of the Moscow legion, from 1769 to 1775

680. Grenadier cap 1769-1775

681. NCO and Officer of the carabinier squadrons of the Moscow legion, from 1769 to 1775

682. Officer and hussar of the Moscow legion, from 1769 to 1775

683. NCO and Officer of the cossack team of the Moscow legion, from 1769 to 1775

684. Royal artillerist of the Moscow legion, from 1769 to 1775

685. Musketeers and NCO light field commands, from 1771 to 1775

686. Artillery man 1771-1775

687. Dragoon and NCO and private light field commands, from 1771 to 1775

688. Dragoon shapka light field commands, from 1771 to 1775

689. Dragoon Officer of the light field commands, from 1771 to 1775

690. Artilleryman light field commands, from 1771 to 1775

691. Fusilier regiment, from 1763 to 1786

692. NCO and fusilier regiment, from 1763 to 1786

693. Officer of the fusilier regiment, from 1763 to 1786

694. Private and drummer of the fusilier regiment, from 1763 to 1786

695. Officer of the kanonirsky regiment, from 1763 to 1786

696. Private of bombardier regiment, from 1763 to 1786

697. Bombardier cap, from 1763 to 1786

698. Generals of the army 1764-1780

699. Cannonier garrison artillery, from 1763 to 1786

700. Officer and master garrison artillery, from 1765 to 1786

Private hussar regiment, from 1763 to 1783

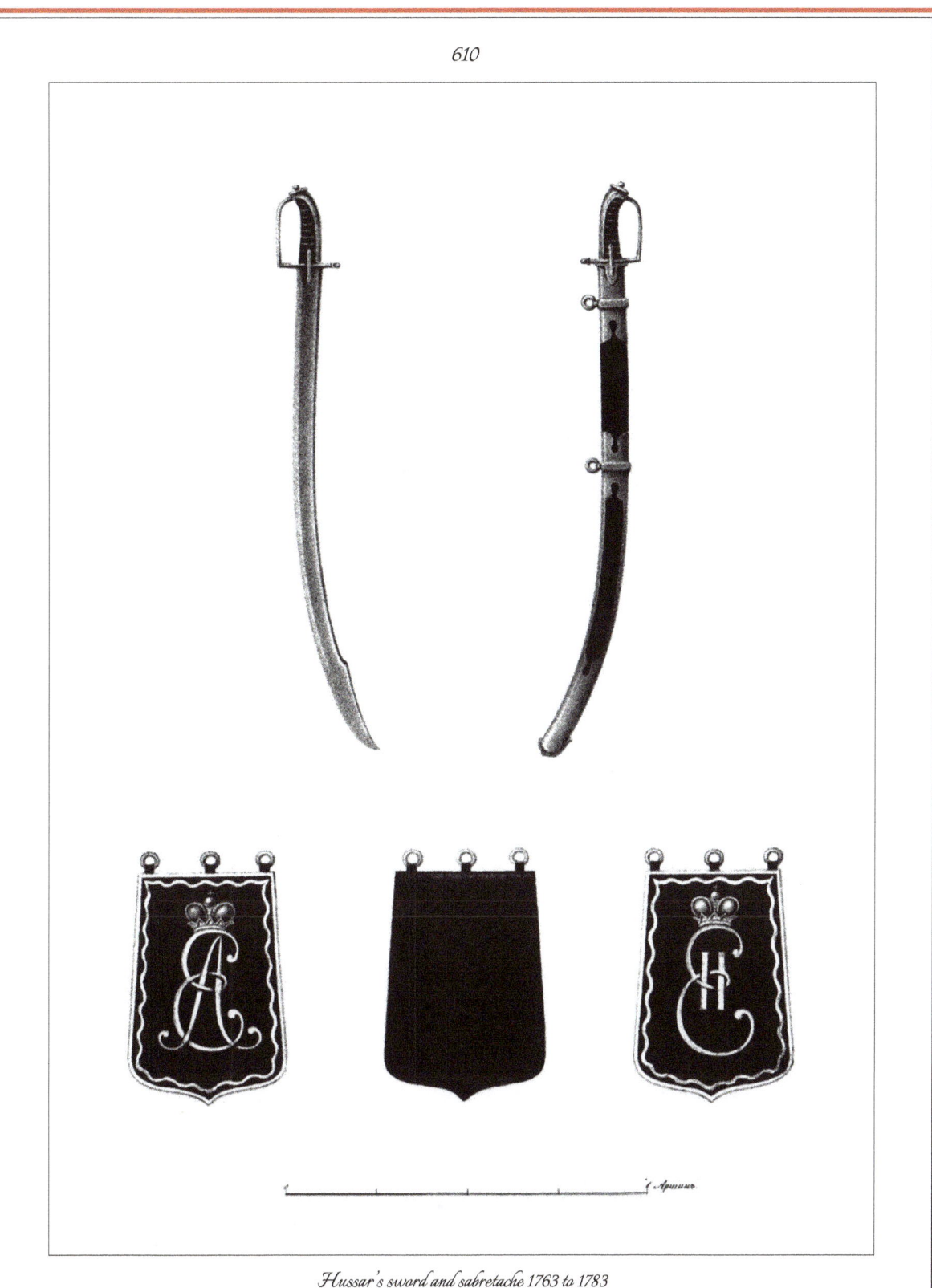

Hussar's sword and sabretache 1763 to 1783

Private hussar regiment, from 1763 to 1776

NCO and Officer of the Serbian hussar regiment, from 1763 to 1776

Trumpet of the Hungarian and Georgian hussars, from 1763 to 1776

Officer of the Georgian hussar regiment, from 1763 to 1776

Officers of the Moldavian hussar regiment, from 1763 to 1776

Officer and Private of black and yellow Georgian hussar regiments, from 1764 to 1776

Bakhmut hussar regiment, from 1764 to 1774

Ostrogozhsky hussar regiment, from 1765 to 1776.

619

Razvoy Izyumsky hussar regiment, from 1765 to 1776

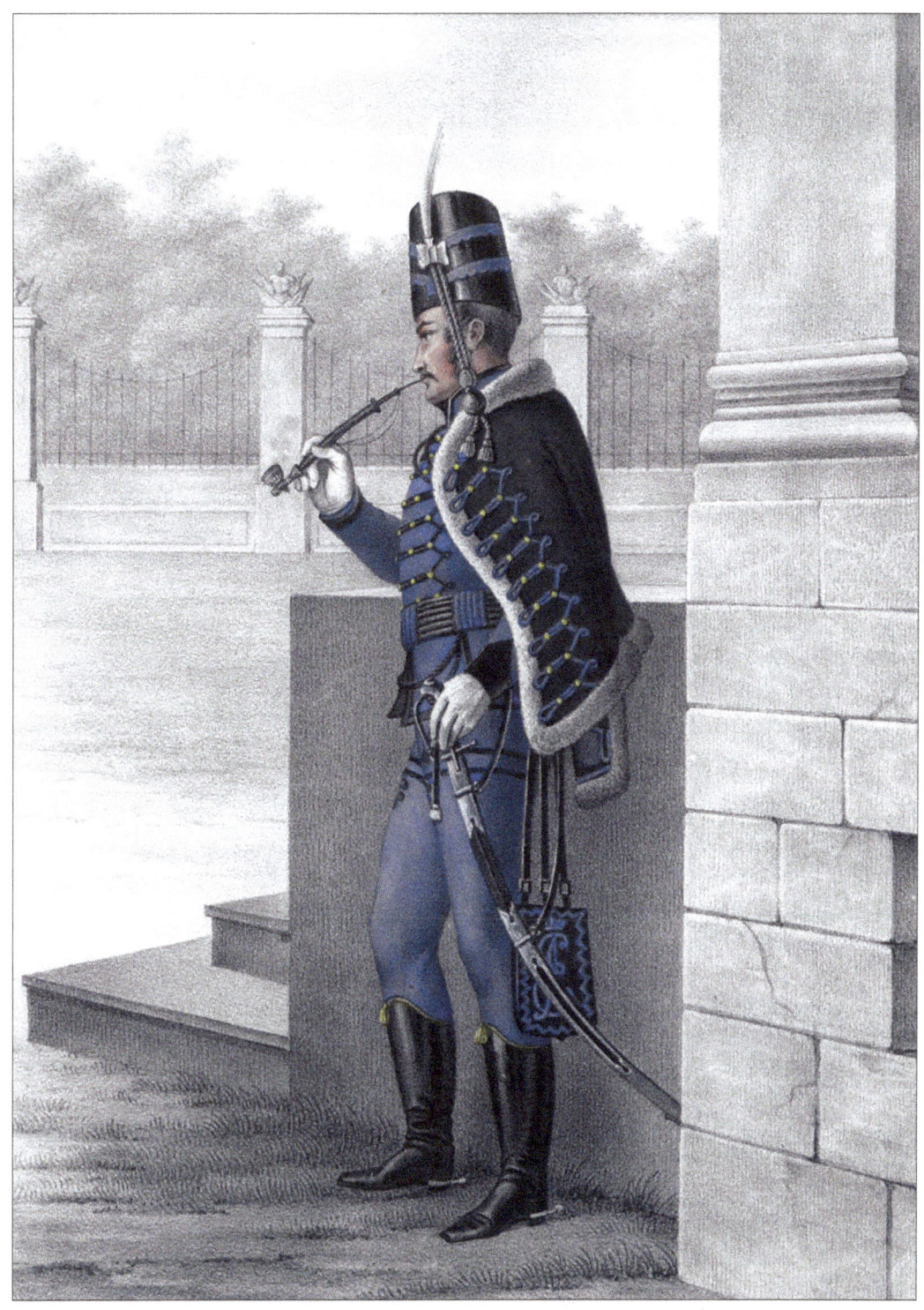

Private of the Sumy hussar regiment, from 1765 to 1776

High Officer of the Sumy hussar regiment, from 1765 to 1776

Private and staff Officer of Kharkov and private and Officer of the Akhtyrsky hussar regiments, from 1765 to 1776

NCO of the Ostrogozhsky hussar regiment, from 1776 to 1783

Officer of the Ostrogozhsky hussar regiment, from 1776 to 1783

625

High Officer and cadet of the Kharkov hussar regiment, from 1776 to 1783

NCO Akhtyrsky hussar regiment, from 1776 to 1783

Private and Officer of the Sumy hussar regiment, from 1776 to 1783.

Cabby Infantry Regiment from 1763 to 1786.

Colonel of the Belarusian hussar regiment, from 1776 to 1783

Ukrainian hussar regiment, from 1776 to 1783

Private of the Hungarian hussar regiment, from 1776 to 1783

Corporal of the Slavonic hussar regiment, from 1776 to 1783

Hussar officer 1776-1783

Cadet of the Moldavian hussar regiment, from 1776 to 1783

Macedonian hussar regiment, from 1776 to 1783

Dalmatsky trumpet and the Illyric hussar regiment, from 1776 to 1783

NCO of the Serbian hussar regiment, from 1776 to 1783

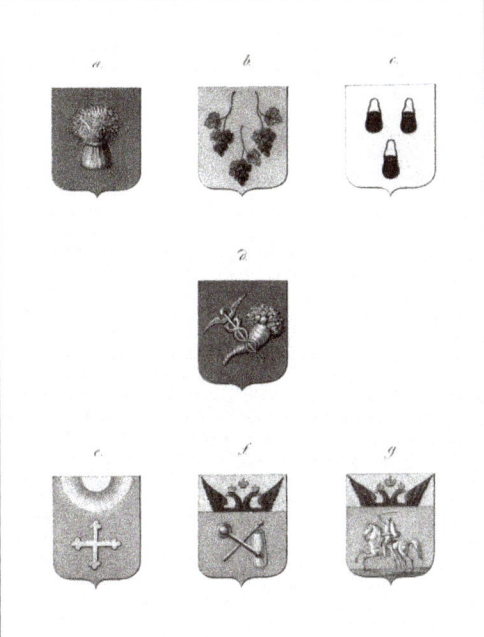

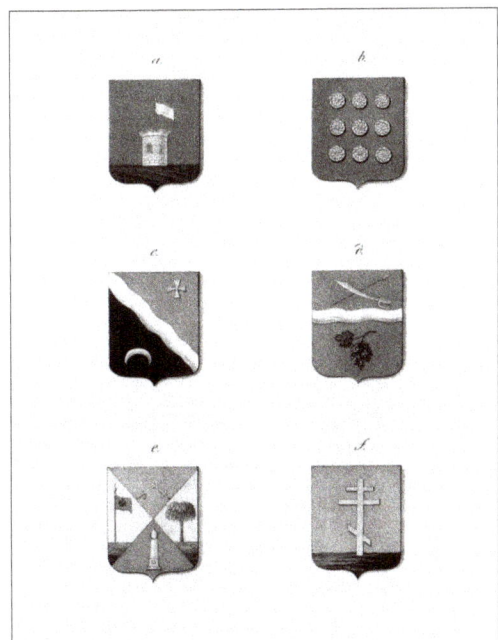

Coats of arms of the field and settlement hussars, from 1776 to 1783 - Coats of arms of the pikemen regiments, from 1776 to 1784 -

Officer and private of the Voronezh hussar regiment, from 1788 to 1796

Regional Holyopolis hussar regiment, from 1788 to 1796

An hussar of line squadrons under the Pskov dragoon regiment, from 1788 to 1796

Moscow muscovite squadron from 1788 to 1796

Horse rider Elizavetgrad pikemen regiment, from 1764 to 1776

Private of the lugansk pikemen regiment, from 1764 to 1776

Quartermaster of the Dnieper pikemen regiment, from 1764 to 1776

Private of the Donetsk pikemen regiment, from 1764 to 1776

Trumpet of the Dnieper pikemen regiment, from 1764 to 1776

NCO and Officer of the Donetsk pikemen regiment, from 1764 to 1776

Private of Yekaterinoslav pikemen regiment, from 1776 to 1784

Trumpet and NCO of Elizavetgrad pikinernogo regiment, from 1776 to 1784

Private Kherson and Officer of the Poltava pikemen regiments, from 1776 to 1784

Officer of the Dnieper pikemen regiment, 1776-1784

High Officer of the Lugansk pikemen regiment, from 1776 to 1784

Private and Trumpeter light legged regiments, from 1786 to 1796

Officer of the light-colored regiments, from 1786 to 1796

Officer of light-legged regiments in the army of prince Potemkin, from 1788 to 1792

A horse farmer in 1788

Horse Yegorsky Officer in 1788

Officer from 1789 to 1792 and Private from 1789 to 1796

Horse Yegorsky drummer, from 1790 to 1796

Horse Yegorsky Officer from 1792 to 1796

General mayor and general adjutant field cavalry, from 1764 to 1780

665

Cavalry's generals, from 1780 to 1796

Drummer and musketeers battalions of the St. Petersburg legion, from 1765 to 1775

NCO and Officer of the St. Petersburg legion, from 1769 to 1775

High Officer of the St. Petersburg legion, from 1765 to 1775

Grenadier and a jager of the St. Petersburg legion, from 1769 to 1775

Grenadiers shapki Petersburg and Moscow legions, from 1769 to 1775

Carabiner of the St. Petersburg legion, from 1769 to 1775

Officer and NCO carabinier squadrons of the St. Petersburg legion, from 1769 to 1775

673

Private and NCO hussars squadrons of the st. Petersburg legion from 1765 to 1775

Hussar Officer of the St. Petersburg legion, from 1765 to 1775

NCO of the St. Petersburg legion, from 1769 to 1775

Cossack Officer of the St. Petersburg legion, from 1765 to 1775

Men of artillery, engineering. NCO and the ober-quartermaster of the St. Petersburg legion, from 1769 to 1775

678

Jaeger and musketeer of the Moscow legion, from 1769 to 1775

Grenadiers of the Moscow legion, from 1769 to 1775

Grenadier cap 1769-1775

NCO and Officer of the carabinier squadrons of the Moscow legion, from 1769 to 1775

682

Officer and hussar of the Moscow legion, from 1769 to 1775

NCO and Officer of the cossack team of the Moscow legion, from 1769 to 1775

Royal artillerist of the Moscow legion, from 1769 to 1775

Musketeers and NCO light field commands, from 1771 to 1775

Artillery man 1771-1775

Dragoon and NCO and private light field commands, from 1771 to 1775

Dragoon shapka light field commands, from 1771 to 1775

Dragoon Officer of the light field commands, from 1771 to 1775

Artilleryman light field commands, from 1771 to 1775

Fusilier regiment, from 1763 to 1786

NCO and fusilier regiment, from 1763 to 1786

Officer of the fusilier regiment, from 1763 to 1786

Private and drummer of the fusilier regiment, from 1763 to 1786

Officer of the kanonirsky regiment, from 1763 to 1786

Private of bombardier regiment, from 1763 to 1786

Bombardier cap, from 1763 to 1786

Generals of the army 1764-1780

Cannonier garrison artillery, from 1763 to 1786

Officer an master garrison artillery, from 1765 to 1786

SOLDIERS, WEAPONS & UNIFORMS ALREADY PUBLISHED
(SOME TITLES)

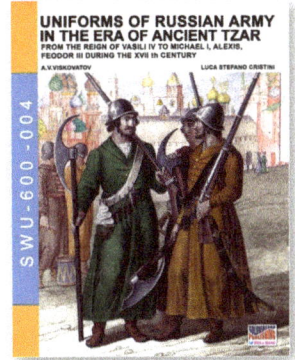

UNIFORMS OF RUSSIAN ARMY IN THE ERA OF ANCIENT TZAR
FROM THE REIGN OF VASILI IV TO MICHAEL I, ALEXIS, FEODOR III DURING THE XVII th CENTURY
A.V.VISKOVATOV   LUCA STEFANO CRISTINI
SWU-600-004

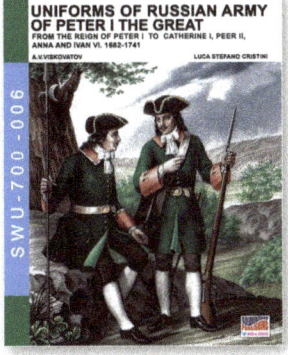

UNIFORMS OF RUSSIAN ARMY OF PETER I THE GREAT
FROM THE REIGN OF PETER I TO CATHERINE I, PEER II, ANNA AND IVAN VI, 1682-1741
A.V.VISKOVATOV   LUCA STEFANO CRISTINI
SWU-700-006

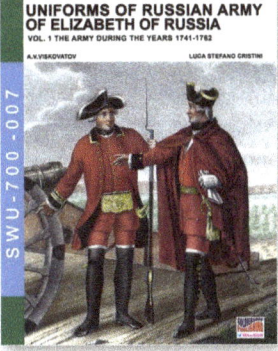

UNIFORMS OF RUSSIAN ARMY OF ELIZABETH OF RUSSIA
VOL. 1 THE ARMY DURING THE YEARS 1741-1762
A.V.VISKOVATOV   LUCA STEFANO CRISTINI
SWU-700-007

UNIFORMS OF RUSSIAN ARMY OF ELIZABETH OF RUSSIA
VOL. 2 THE ARMY DURING THE YEARS 1741-1762
A.V.VISKOVATOV   LUCA STEFANO CRISTINI
SWU-700-008

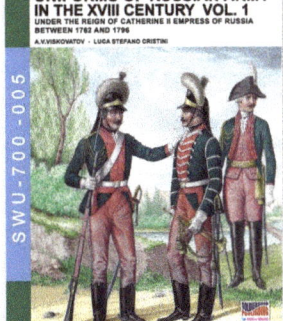

UNIFORMS OF RUSSIAN ARMY IN THE XVIII CENTURY VOL. 1
UNDER THE REIGN OF CATHERINE II EMPRESS OF RUSSIA BETWEEN 1762 AND 1796
A.V.VISKOVATOV - LUCA STEFANO CRISTINI
SWU-700-005

UNIFORMS OF RUSSIAN ARMY IN THE XVIII CENTURY VOL. 2
UNDER THE REIGN OF CATHERINE II EMPRESS OF RUSSIA BETWEEN 1762 AND 1796
A.V.VISKOVATOV - LUCA STEFANO CRISTINI
SWU-700-009

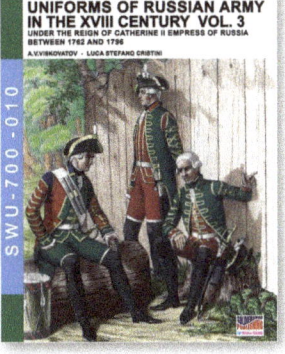

UNIFORMS OF RUSSIAN ARMY IN THE XVIII CENTURY VOL. 3
UNDER THE REIGN OF CATHERINE II EMPRESS OF RUSSIA BETWEEN 1762 AND 1796
A.V.VISKOVATOV - LUCA STEFANO CRISTINI
SWU-700-010

UNIFORMS OF RUSSIAN ARMY IN THE XVIII CENTURY VOL. 4
UNDER THE REIGN OF CATHERINE II EMPRESS OF RUSSIA BETWEEN 1762 AND 1796
A.V.VISKOVATOV - LUCA STEFANO CRISTINI
SWU-700-011

BRITISH ARMY UNIFORMS IN 1742
IN THE ART OF JOHN PINE
SWU-700-001

PRUSSIAN & AUSTRIAN ARMY UNIFORMS IN 1742-1770
LUCA STEFANO CRISTINI
SWU-700-002

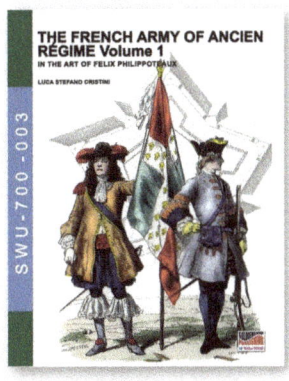

THE FRENCH ARMY OF ANCIEN RÉGIME Volume 1
IN THE ART OF FELIX PHILIPPOTEAUX
LUCA STEFANO CRISTINI
SWU-700-003

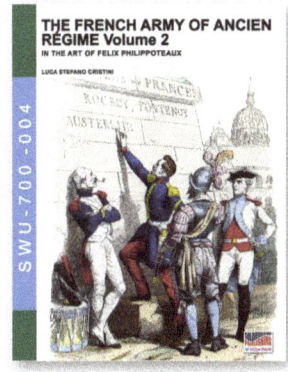

THE FRENCH ARMY OF ANCIEN RÉGIME Volume 2
IN THE ART OF FELIX PHILIPPOTEAUX
LUCA STEFANO CRISTINI
SWU-700-004

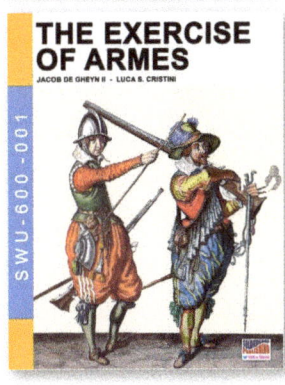

THE EXERCISE OF ARMES
JACOB DE GHEYN II - LUCA S. CRISTINI
SWU-600-001

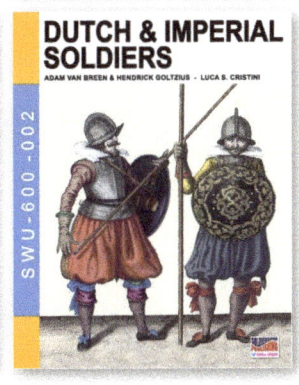

DUTCH & IMPERIAL SOLDIERS
ADAM VAN BREEN & HENDRICK GOLTZIUS - LUCA S. CRISTINI
SWU-600-002

HORSEMEN IN THE 16TH & 17TH C.
JACOB DE GHEYN II - A.DE BRUYN - LUCA S. CRISTINI
SWU-600-003

IMPERIAL SOLDIERS & UNIFORMS 1640-1860
IN THE ART OF FRANZ GERASCH
LUCA S.CRISTINI   Plates by FRANZ GERASCH
SWU-GEN-001

www.ingramcontent.com/pod-product-compliance
Lightning Source LLC
Chambersburg PA
CBHW041143120626
46547CB00020B/3087